# Diet recommendations for Hyperuricaemia and Gout

Please check these recommendations always with a nutrition consultant, therapist, doctor or dietician. The recipes and the list of ingredients are supporting the conventional medical therapy.
The calorie disclosures of fresh ingredients (fruit and vegetables) vary according to quality and time of harvest. The contents were checked by a dietician and a nutrition consultant for the Traditional Chinese Medicine (TCM).

Author:
©2019 Josef Miligui
www.ebns.at

AF206285

Source:
The lists are created from the EBNS database for nutritional counseling. The database is used by dietitians, therapists and doctors for advising the patient / client.

Literature:
The specialist literature and the training documents of the German and Austrian dietary and traditional Chinese medicine serve as a knowledge base. We have used the documents as a basis of knowledge, adapted it to our experience and completed them.
http://di-book.com

Production and publishing:
BoD – Books on Demand, Norderstedt
ISBN: 9783746098401

# Diet recommendations for DIETETICS - Metabolism - Hyperuricaemia and Gout

# 1   Treatment strategy

Purine reduced diet <300 mg uric acid per day (2,000 mg per week)
- Avoid alcohol
- Normalize the weight
- Ovolactovegetarian diet (Ovo = egg, lacto = milk, dairy products)

- If there is no other regulation, drink enough (at least 2 liters per day)!
Milk and milk products as well as eggs are purin-free or purin-poor.
They are particularly suitable as a protein source since pure protein
promotes uric acid excretion via the kidney.
Whole grain products are purin-poor and therefore suitable!
Purine-free or purine-poor foods containing purine in a form which is not
metabolized to uric acid: Vegetables, potatoes, fruit, noodles, rice,
bread, dairy products.
Beverages: fruit juices, vegetable juices, cocoa, coffee, milk, mineral
water, tea.

# 2  Avoid

Fat dishes, legumes, meat extracts, heart, veal liver, kidney, liver
sausage, fish (smoked), fish preserves, herring, anchovies, caviar,
chocolate, yeast extract, alcoholic beverages, mainly beer.
Since a high protein content of foodstuffs is usually also associated with
a high purine content, it should be avoided sparingly with protein-rich
foods.

These foods contain a lot of purine.
Meat and sausage in general, especially veal broth, liver and other offal,
meat broths.
Sardines, sardines, salmon, shrimp, herring, mackerel, trout, clams,
carp, carp, sole, tuna, cod, curative.
Baker's press yeast and products made therefrom, meat extract.

# 3  Breakfast

|  | kkal. per serving |
|---|---|
| Apple - banana cream | 110 |
| Barley mash with plums | 106 |
| Barley mash with steamed pear | 113 |
| Boiled celery salad with exotic spices | 165 |
| Breakfast - Rice with fruits | 230 |
| Breakfast with cheese | 593 |
| Broccoli and Parmesan spread on toast bread | 148 |
| Carrot and potato rucola sandwich | 94 |
| Coffee | 16 |
| Colorful rice dish | 437 |
| Compote from plums | 22 |
| Compote from rhubarb | 48 |

# 4 Snack

# 5 Lunch

# 6  Afternoon

# 7 Dinner

# 8   Any time

# 9 Recipes

(rec.) = You can use more.
(little) = You should use less than specified
(no) omit.

## 9.1 Antipasti

Improves blood circulation, anti-inflammatory, relieves pain. Diuretic, promotes digestion, reduces blood pressure, antioxidative, antibacterial, affects anorexia, improves digestion, flatulence, stomach weakness, stimulating.
Cooking time approx. 40 min

3 portions to 246,67g. / 100kcal. - (carb:54% / prot:46%)
100g.=40,54kcal. / protein 2,74g. fat:5,6g.
μg. - Ph:7,93 Na:1,08 Ka:67,54 Mg:5,14 Ca:7,21 Fe:0,24 Zn:0,03 Col.:0 Hsr.:5,8

**Quantity of ingredients:**
Pepperoni 1 piece / 5g. (yes)
Lemon juice 1 table spoon / 10g. (yes)
Aubergine 1 piece / 300g. (yes)
Tomato 4 pieces / 200g. (yes)
Zucchini 5/8 oz / 200g. (yes)
Lemon peel 1/2 piece / 3g. (yes)
Olive oil 1 table spoon / 15g. (yes)
Basil (fresh) 8 leaves / 5g. (yes)
Salt 1 pinch / 0,5g. (little)
Coriander 1/2 teaspoon / 2g. (yes)

**Cooking instructions:**
Preheat the oven to 250 degrees Celsius and bake the hot peppers until the bowl becomes dark (about 20 minutes). Cover the hot peppers with a clear film and allow to cool. Peel the skin and cut into strips about 2 cm wide. Cut tomatoes in half and spread with oil in slices of aubergine and bake in the oven at 200 degrees golden brown (about 10 minutes) Fry the zucchini slices in the grill pan (without fat).
Mix everything together, mix the marinade of olive oil, salt and lemon peel and pour over the vegetables, sprinkle with coriander. Leave for 1 hour.

## 9.2 Apple - banana cream

Regulates gastrointestinal function, provides vitamin C, cholesterol lowering, reduces inflammation, diuretic, improves blood circulation.
Cooking time approx. 15 min
4 portions to 206,25g. / 110kcal. - (carb:94% / prot:6%)
100g.=53,45kcal. / protein 0,84g. fat:0,51g.
µg. - Ph:0,75 Na:0,12 Ka:9,5 Mg:0,68 Ca:0,56 Fe:0,03 Zn:0,01 Col.:0 Hsr.:0,8

**Quantity of ingredients:**
Apple (sour) 7/8 lbs / 400g. (yes)
Water 3/4 cup - 6 oz / 200g. (yes)
Orange peel 1/4 piece / 5g. (yes)
Lemon peel 1/2 piece / 2g. (yes)
Sugar brown 2 teaspoons / 6g. (little)
Cinnamon sticks 1 piece / 0g. (yes)
Banana 1 piece / 150g. (yes)
Acerola fruit nectar or powder 1 teaspoon / 2g. (little)
Orange juice 1/2 piece / 50g. (little)
Lemon juice 1 table spoon / 10g. (yes)

**Cooking instructions:**
Cut the apple into fine slices, bring water to boil and add the apple slices, orange- and lemon peel, sugar and cinnamon and simmer about 7 minutes. The apples should be almost soft. Remove acerola and the cinnamon stick. Mix the apple, the banana, the orange juice and the lemon juice.

## 9.3 Apricot and cranberry ice cream

Forces resistance to infections, good to fight oral mucosal inflammation, diarrhea. Has a positive effect on the urinary tract.
Cooking time approx. 5 min
2 portions to 222,5g. / 106kcal. - (carb:91% / prot:9%)
100g.=47,87kcal. / protein 1,9g. fat:0,48g.
µg. - Ph:7,98 Na:0,94 Ka:107,17 Mg:4,69 Ca:8,02 Fe:0,03 Zn:0 Col.:0 Hsr.:8,57

**Quantity of ingredients:**
Apricots 3/4 lbs / 350g. (yes)
Water 1/4 cup / 50g. (yes)
Cranberry 3 table spoons / 45g. (yes)

**Cooking instructions:**
Mix the apricot juice with the cranberry syrup. Fill the juice into little molds, place in the freezer and let it freeze in about 3 hours.

## 9.4 Asparagus Cream Soup

Diuretic, improves blood circulation, prevents cancer, laxative, antiparasitic, stimulates liver function, good to fight loss of appetite, flatulence, rheumatism, heartburn.
Cooking time approx. 45 min
Allergens: ACG
2 portions to 409,5g. / 240kcal. - (carb:21% / prot:79%)
100g.=58,61kcal. / protein 5,2g. fat:19,85g.
µg. - Ph:9,44 Na:1,5 Ka:15,8 Mg:1,6 Ca:6,23 Fe:0,13 Zn:0,08 Col.:9,84 Hsr.:2,42

**Quantity of ingredients:**
Asparagus (green or white) 5/8 oz / 200g. (yes)
Water 2 cup / 500g. (yes)
Rapeseed oil 3 table spoons / 30g. (yes)
Wheat flour 2 table spoons / 10g. (yes)
Chicken yolk 1 piece / 25g. (yes)
Cow's milk (whole milk 3.5% fat) 1 table spoon / 15g. (yes)
Sour cream 15% fat 1 table spoon / 15g. (little)
Pepper (ground) 1 pinch / 0,5g. ()
Nutmeg 1 pinch / 0,5g. (yes)
Lemon juice 1 teaspoon / 2g. (yes)
Parsley 2 table spoons / 20g. (yes)
Salt 1 pinch / 1g. (little)

**Cooking instructions:**
Wash and peel the asparagus.
Heat water, a little lemon juice and pinch of salt till it boils. Tie the asparagus spears together.
Add the asparagus peel to the cooking water and bring to the boil.
Add the asparagus and cook on low heat for about 20 minutes.
Then remove the asparagus bunches and pour the broth through a sieve.
For the roux, heat the oil in a saucepan, add the flour and sauté until it is colorless, slowly top up with the asparagus sauce and simmer for 10 minutes. Cut the asparagus spears into pieces about 3 cm long and place them to the soup.

Just before serving, bring the soup to the boil again.
Mix the egg yolk with the milk and sour cream.
Remove the pot from the heat and stir in the egg yolk and milk mixture.
Season with pepper and nutmeg, decorate with the chopped parsley and serve immediately.

## 9.5 Barley mash with plums

Promotes spleen, diuretic, forcing spleen, supports urination, relaxes, reduces internal heat.
Cooking time approx. 25 min
Allergens: AG
5 portions to 289,6g. / 107kcal. - (carb:81% / prot:19%)
100g.=36,88kcal. / protein 3,15g. fat:1,57g.
µg. - Ph:1,2 Na:0,1 Ka:2,2 Mg:0,44 Ca:0,34 Fe:0,01 Zn:0,01 Col.:0,04 Hsr.:0,42

**Quantity of ingredients:**
Water 10 cups / 1200g. (yes)
Barley 1 cup / 120g. (yes)
Plum 1 cup / 120g. (yes)
Butter organic 2 teaspoons / 6g. (little)
Sugar cane sugar 1/2 teaspoon / 2g. (little)

**Cooking instructions:**
Grind coarse the barley and roast it dry. Add hot water, add ginger and cardamom and let it swell to a pulp in low heat. Core the plums and boil for 10 minutes with a little water. At the end, add the stewed plums, a little butter and sweetener.

Variant: If you want to go fast, you can use barley flakes instead of shot.

## 9.6 Barley mash with steamed pear

Promotes digestion, supports urination, promotes spleen, diuretic, forcing spleen, relaxes, promotes perspiration.
Cooking time approx. 25 min
Allergens: A
5 portions to 305,8g. / 114kcal. - (carb:86% / prot:14%)
100g.=37,21kcal. / protein 3,26g. fat:0,72g.
µg. - Ph:1,16 Na:0,11 Ka:2,09 Mg:0,44 Ca:0,33 Fe:0,01 Zn:0,01 Col.:0 Hsr.:0,42

**Quantity of ingredients:**
Water 10 cups / 1200g. (yes)
Barley 1 cup / 120g. (yes)
Ginger fresh 2 slices / 2g. (yes)
Cardamom 3 capsules / 1g. (yes)
Salt 1 pinch / 1g. (little)
Pear 1 piece / 200g. (yes)
Sugar cane sugar 1/2 teaspoon / 5g. (little)

**Cooking instructions:**
Grind coarse the barley and roast it dry. Add hot water, add ginger and cardamom and let it swell to a pulp in low heat. Peel and dice the pear and boil for 10 minutes with a little water. At the end, add the stewed pear, a little butter and sweetener.

Variant: If you want to go fast, you can use barley flakes instead of shot.

## 9.7 Basic recipe for a chicken broth worming

Strengthens blood, strengthens bone marrow, reduces blood pressure, strengthens immune system, prevents cancer, reduces radiation damage, promotes sweating, dissolves stagnation, good to fight loss of appetite, flatulence.
Cooking time approx. 2-3 hours
Allergens: L
9 portions to 244,89g. / 90kcal. - (carb:10% / prot:90%)
100g.=36,66kcal. / protein 15,68g. fat:11,56g.
µg. - Ph:0,86 Na:0,59 Ka:1,87 Mg:0,13 Ca:0,38 Fe:0,01 Zn:0 Col.:0,25 Hsr.:0,92

**Quantity of ingredients:**
Chicken meat 1/2 piece / 600g. (yes)
Carrot 2 pieces / 150g. (yes)
Leek 1 stick / 45g. (yes)
Celery root 1 piece / 500g. (yes)
Ginger fresh 2 slices / 2g. (yes)
Fenugreek (Trigonella foenum-graecum) 1 teaspoon / 2g. (yes)
Juniper berry 1 teaspoon / 3g. (yes)
Bay leaf 3 pieces / 2g. (yes)
Water 4 cup / 900g. (yes)

**Cooking instructions:**
Remove chicken parts from fat. Place chicken pieces in a saucepan with hot water and heat till it boils briefly, skimming any resulting foam. Add coarsely chopped vegetables and all spices and cook over medium heat for 2 to 3 hours. Strain the finished soup. Throw away vegetables and bones.
Tip: If you want to use the meat as a soup insert, take out after 45 minutes and return only the bones in the soup.
Refrigerate for later use.

## 9.8 Basic recipe for a reissue soup (Congee)

Low fat content, for the drainage of the body overweight and high blood pressure.
Cooking time approx. 2-4 hours
3 portions to 273,33g. / 140kcal. - (carb:90% / prot:10%)
100g.=51,34kcal. / protein 2,96g. fat:0,48g.
µg. - Ph:1,95 Na:0,19 Ka:1,67 Mg:1,14 Ca:0,57 Fe:0,01 Zn:0,02 Col.:0 Hsr.:2,11

**Quantity of ingredients:**
Rice variety any 1 cup / 120g. (yes)
Water 6 cups / 700g. (yes)

**Cooking instructions:**
Cook rice and water in a ratio of about 1: 6. The amount of water determines the thickness of the mash (matter of taste).
Put the rice in a saucepan with a heavy lid. It is important to simmer the rice after a short boil on the slightest flame, otherwise it burns.
Boil the rice for 2-4 hours. The longer he cooks, the more he strengthens.
If you want to eat the dish for breakfast, you can put the rice on just before bedtime.
To be on the safe side, you should first check the behavior of your pot and cooker under observation for a similar amount of time, so that nothing burns.
Refrigerate for later use.

## 9.9 Basic recipe for a vegetable soup, nutritious

Reduces blood pressure, strengthens immune system, prevents cancer, forcing spleen, dissolves stagnation, promotes weight loss. Good to fight immunodeficiency, high blood pressure, depressions, diabetes, diarrhea, reduces blood lipids.
Cooking time approx. 2-3 hours
Allergens: L
5 portions to 240,6g. / 48kcal. - (carb:71% / prot:29%)
100g.=19,87kcal. / protein 1,56g. fat:1,31g.
µg. - Ph:0,97 Na:0,73 Ka:5,14 Mg:0,36 Ca:1,26 Fe:0,02 Zn:0,01 Col.:0 Hsr.:0,56

**Quantity of ingredients:**
Olive oil 1 table spoon / 4g. (yes)
Onion white 1 piece / 60g. (yes)
Carrot 3 pieces / 200g. (yes)
Parsnip 3/8 lbs - 6oz / 150g. (yes)
Celery root 1 cup / 100g. (yes)

Ginger fresh 1/2 teaspoon / 2g. (yes)
Lemon 1/2 piece / 25g. (yes)
Juniper berry 6 pieces / 6g. (yes)
Thyme dried 1 pinch / 1g. (yes)
Lovage 1 table spoon / 3g. (yes)
Bay leaf 2 leaves / 1g. (yes)
Salt 1 pinch / 1g. (little)
Water 3 cups / 650g. (yes)

**Cooking instructions:**
Cut the vegetables into cubes.
Heat oil in hot pot, fry shortly onions and vegetables.
Add cold water, then add ginger, bay leaf and lemon juice.
Season with juniper, thyme and lovage. Cover for 2 - 3 hours on a low heat and simmer.
The used vegetables should be thrown away.
The basic recipe serves as a soup base and to refine vegetables, legumes or cereals.
If you want to eat vegetable soup immediately, add the desired vegetables half an hour before.
Refrigerate for later use.

# 9.10 Basmati rice + Zucchini tofu dish

Diuretic, supports urination, harmonizes spleen and stomach, reduces flatulence, good to fight body overweight and high blood pressure.
Antioxidative, promotes digestion, perspiration, reduces blood lipids, forcing spleen.
Cooking time approx. 20 min
Allergens: E
4 portions to 306,75g. / 146kcal. - (carb:57% / prot:43%)
100g.=47,51kcal. / protein 7,95g. fat:4,89g.
µg. - Ph:13,21 Na:0,7 Ka:33,77 Mg:10,99 Ca:11,98 Fe:0,34 Zn:0,02 Col.:0 Hsr.:7,75

**Quantity of ingredients:**
Soy Tofu 5/8 lbs - 8oz / 250g. (yes)
Olive oil 2 table spoons / 6g. (yes)
Coriander 1/2 teaspoon / 4g. (yes)
Ginger fresh 1/2 teaspoon / 4g. (yes)
Rice Basmati 1/2 cup / 60g. (yes)
Water 3 cups / 200g. (yes)
Zucchini 1 piece / 700g. (yes)

**Cooking instructions:**

Cut tofu cubes and marinate with olive oil, tamari, crushed coriander and ginger. Leave at least 1 hour.

Cook Basmati rice with the water. You can season with onion and cardamom.

Roast zucchini and tofu in pan in the hot oil for approx. 5-7 min.

Serve rice and tofu on a plate.

Add the parsley.

Can also be used as a salad for the home and on the go.

## 9.11 Beef pumpkin and vegetable stew

Reduces inflammation, improves digestion, reduces blood glucose, strengthens the muscles, promotes digestion, helps to digest fat.

Cooking time approx. 1 hour

Allergens: AL

4 portions to 403,75g. / 369kcal. - (carb:48% / prot:52%)
100g.=91,46kcal. / protein 30,38g. fat:11,37g.
µg. - Ph:4,56 Na:3,23 Ka:16,05 Mg:1,7 Ca:3,71 Fe:0,08 Zn:0,08 Col.:1 Hsr.:2,83

**Quantity of ingredients:**

Beef meat 3/4 lbs / 350g. (yes)

Pumpkin 3/4 lbs / 350g. (yes)

Leek 3/8 lbs - 6oz / 150g. (yes)

Potato 3/4 lbs / 350g. (yes)

Tomato 3/8 lbs - 6oz / 150g. (yes)

Olive oil 2 table spoons / 25g. (yes)

Basic recipe for a vegetable soup (nutritious) 1/4 lbs - 4oz / 125g. (yes)

Salt 1 pinch / 1g. (little)

Pepper (ground) 1 pinch / 0,5g. ()

Ground caraway 1 pinch / 1g. (yes)

Sugar cane sugar 1 pinch / 1g. (little)

Parsley 1/2 bunch / 30g. (yes)

White bread (wheat bread) 4 slices / 80g. (little)

**Cooking instructions:**

Dice beef. Peel pumpkin and dice. Cut the leek into rings and dice the peeled potatoes.

Brew the tomatoes with boiling water, peel off the skin and dice.

Steam the meat in olive oil and fill with vegetable stock. Add the cleaned vegetables. Season with salt, pepper, paprika, cumin and fructose. Stew for 30 minutes over low heat.

Season again and sprinkle with parsley and serve with white bread.

## 9.12 Beef salad

Strengths spleen and stomach, strengthens blood, strengthens the muscles, tendons and bones, diuretic, detoxifying, suppresses conversion of sugar into fat, lowers cholesterol, dissolves stagnation.
Cooking time approx. 10 min
Allergens: O
1 portion to 197g. / 249kcal. - (carb:54% / prot:46%)
100g.=126,4kcal. / protein 15,71g. fat:7,9g.
µg. - Ph:151,93 Na:219,82 Ka:142,62 Mg:14,06 Ca:28,43 Fe:1,3 Zn:1,53 Col.:18,53 Hsr.:43,25

**Quantity of ingredients:**
Beef meat 1/8 lbs - 2oz / 50g. (yes)
Onion white 1/2 oz / 20g. (yes)
Peppers 1 oz / 30g. (yes)
Cucumber (spicy cucumber) 1 oz / 30g. (yes)
Vinegar (Apple vinegar) 2 teaspoons / 5g. (yes)
Rapeseed oil 2 teaspoons / 5g. (yes)
Salt 1 pinch / 0,5g. (little)
Pepper (ground) 1 pinch / 0,1g. ()
Chives 1 table spoon / 7g. (yes)
Bread with carob kernel flour 2 slices / 50g. (yes)

**Cooking instructions:**
Cook the meat with the basic recipe of a beef broth and let it cool down. Cut into 1 cm slices. Cut the onions into rings, pepper and gherkin into small cubes. Mix all ingredients. Make the salad marinade with vinegar, oil and salt and pour over, season to taste and strain.

## 9.13 Boiled celery salad with exotic spices

Forcing spleen, relieves diarrhea, antibacterial, blood-forming, blood detoxifying, reduces inflammation, diuretic, improves blood circulation.
Cooking time approx. 30 min
Allergens: GLMNO
4 portions to 341g. / 166kcal. - (carb:48% / prot:52%)
100g.=48,61kcal. / protein 5,59g. fat:9,17g.
µg. - Ph:3,39 Na:6,17 Ka:17,47 Mg:0,76 Ca:5,05 Fe:0,03 Zn:0,01 Col.:0,2 Hsr:3,02

**Quantity of ingredients:**
Celery root 1 1/2 piece / 900g. (yes)
Yogurt (natural, 3.5% fat) 1 cup / 250g. (yes)
Sour cream 15% fat 2 table spoons / 20g. (little)
Turmeric (yellow root) 1 pinch / 1g. (yes)

Sesame oil 1 table spoon / 20g. (yes)
Pepper (ground) 1 pinch / 0,5g. ()
Lemongrass 1 pinch / 1g. (yes)
Onion white 1/2 piece / 25g. (yes)
Mustard 1/2 teaspoon / 1g. (yes)
Black caraway 1 pinch / 1g. (yes)
Salt 1 pinch / 1g. (little)
Lemon juice 1 piece / 40g. (yes)
Apple (sour) 1/2 piece / 100g. (yes)
Peppers powder 1 pinch / 1g. (yes)
Vinegar (Apple vinegar) 1 dash / 3g. (yes)

**Cooking instructions:**
Cook the peeled celeriac in thick slices and then cut into bite-sized strips.
Dressing: Mix a little yoghurt, sour cream, turmeric, sesame oil, pepper, lemongrass powder, finely chopped onion, a little mustard, salt, crushed black cumin, some cold water, lemon juice or vinegar; add the sour chopped apple, some rose paprika, the lukewarm celery and mix well; let it rest for 2 - 3 hours or overnight.
Ideal as a substitute for raw food

## 9.14 Breakfast - Rice with fruits

Good to fight blood circulation disorders, thrombose, risk of embolism, high blood pressure, a headache, heart attack and stroke. Encourages blood build-up, promotes digestion, reduces Inflammation.
Cooking time approx. 10 min - 3 hours
Allergens: GHO
3 portions to 282g. / 231kcal. - (carb:90% / prot:10%)
100g.=81,8kcal. / protein 3,59g. fat:7,61g.
µg. - Ph:3,19 Na:0,7 Ka:8,57 Mg:20,72 Ca:21,22 Fe:0,05 Zn:0,02 Col.:0,54 Hsr.:0,92

**Quantity of ingredients:**
Basic recipe for a rice soup (Congee) 6 cups / 500g. (yes)
Cow's milk (whole milk 3.5% fat) 1/2 to 1 cup / 80g. (yes)
Honey 1 table spoon / 10g. (little)
Butter organic 1 table spoon / 15g. (little)
Dates dried 1 table spoon / 15g. (little)
Fig 1 table spoon / 15g. (yes)
Apple (sour) 1 piece / 200g. (yes)
Hazelnuts 1/2 teaspoon / 5g. (yes)
Almond 1/2 teaspoon / 5g. (yes)
Cinnamon ground 1 pinch / 1g. (yes)

**Cooking instructions:**
Cook rice congee according to basic recipe or use pre-cooked.
Make it with the milk more fluid, and sweet with honey.
Fry the fruits and nuts in butter and mix with the finished rice soup, add chopped dates, figs and the apple.

## 9.15 Breakfast with cheese

Good to fight weakness, stomach pressure, belching, diabetes, acute or chronic obstruction of the bowel, skin problems. Coffee supports urinating, stimulates appetite, detoxifying, increases blood glucose levels, harmonizes heart rhythm.
Cooking time approx. 10 min
Allergens: AGO
1 portion to 364g. / 593kcal. - (carb:46% / prot:54%)
100g.=162,91kcal. / protein 22,49g. fat:34,96g.
µg. - Ph:139,8 Na:214,1 Ka:121 Mg:21,93 Ca:99,75 Fe:0,82 Zn:1,12 Col.:10,93 Hsr.:18,97

**Quantity of ingredients:**
Water 1 cup / 120g. (yes)
Coffee 2 teaspoons / 4g. (yes)
Whole grain bread 2 slices / 100g. (yes)
Margarine 1/2 oz / 10g. (little)
Edam cheese 1 oz / 30g. (yes)
Strawberry jam 1/2 oz / 20g. (little)
Curd cheese 20% 1/8 lbs - 2oz / 40g. (yes)

**Cooking instructions:**
Prepare coffee as usual. Avoid sugar or use sweetener. Cover the bread slices with margarine and put the cheese and marmalade on the breakfast table. Decorating decoratively increases your appetite.

## 9.16 Broccoli and Parmesan spread on toast bread

Good to fight loss of appetite, blood clotting, thyroid function, increase Vitamin B12, strengthen immune system, good to fight belching, diabetes, acute or chronic constipation, dissolves stagnation.
Cooking time approx. 15 min
Allergens: AG
2 portions to 170,5g. / 148kcal. - (carb:29% / prot:71%)
100g.=86,8kcal. / protein 12,1g. fat:11,33g.
µg. - Ph:34,79 Na:27,37 Ka:60,2 Mg:5,76 Ca:40,04 Fe:0,24 Zn:0,19 Col.:1,88 Hsr.:6,09

**Quantity of ingredients:**
Broccoli 5/8 oz / 200g. (yes)
Curd cheese 20% 3 oz / 80g. (yes)
Yogurt (natural, 1.5% fat) 1 table spoon / 10g. (yes)
Parmesan 2 table spoons / 15g. (little)
Lemon peel 1/2 teaspoon / 1g. (yes)
Basil (fresh) 1 table spoon / 5g. (yes)
Chives 1 table spoon / 5g. (yes)
Salt 1 pinch / 1g. (little)
Pepper (ground) 1 pinch / 0,3g. ()
Toast bread (whole grain) 6 slices / 24g. (yes)

**Cooking instructions:**
Cook broccoli in a sieve insert over steam for 8 minutes until firm. Finely chop broccoli.
Mix the curd, yoghurt, parmesan and lemon peel well. Mix cheese cream with broccoli, basil and chives. Season the spread with salt and pepper. Serve on the crunchy toasted toast.

## 9.17 Carrot and millet bake with apple compote

Promotes spleen and liver, reduces blood pressure, strengthens immune system, prevents cancer, reduces radiation damage, calms nerves and stomach, diuretic, good to fight chronic constipation of the intestine.
Cooking time approx. 1 hour
Allergens: CGH
7 portions to 347,86g. / 350kcal. - (carb:64% / prot:36%)
100g.=100,53kcal. / protein 12,54g. fat:12,54g.
µg. - Ph:1,79 Na:0,66 Ka:2,7 Mg:0,54 Ca:1,07 Fe:0,03 Zn:0,01 Col.:0,83 Hsr.:0,28

**Quantity of ingredients:**
Millet 5/8 oz / 200g. (yes)
Cow's milk (whole milk 3.5% fat) 2 cups / 450g. (yes)
Lemon peel 1/2 piece / 2g. (yes)
Sugar brown 2 table spoons / 20g. (little)
Carrot 7/8 lbs / 400g. (yes)
Ginger fresh 2 teaspoons / 6g. (yes)
Acerola fruit nectar or powder 1 teaspoon / 2g. (little)
Almond puree 1/8 lbs - 2oz / 50g. (yes)
Chicken egg 4 pieces / 240g. (yes)
Yogurt (natural, 1.5% fat) 3/8 lbs - 6oz / 150g. (yes)
Butter organic 1 teaspoon / 4g. (little)
Apple (sour) 4 pieces / 600g. (yes)

Water 1 cup / 300g. (yes)
Clove 2 pieces / 1g. (yes)
Sugar brown 1 table spoon / 10g. (little)

**Cooking instructions:**
Preheat the oven to 100°C/212°F (with circulating air 80°C/176°F, gas level 2).
Heat the milk with the millet till it boils, add lemon zest and sugar. Cover and simmer for 5 minutes, then simmer in a preheated oven for 20 minutes. Switch oven to medium heat.
Peel apples and cut into small pieces, boil with water, cloves and sugar for about 5 minutes.
Mix the millet in a bowl with the grated carrots, finely chopped ginger and acerola.
Mix the almond paste (or butter) with the hand mixer. Add egg yolk and stir everything to a smooth cream. Mix in sour cream. Add millet and carrots.
Beat the egg whites very stiff and lift them under the millet pulp. Brush out a baking dish with butter. Add the millet and bake in a preheated oven for 45 minutes on a low heat.
Serve with the apple compote.

## 9.18 Carrot and potato rucola sandwich

Reduces inflammation, improves digestion, supports urination, lowers cholesterol, strengthens immune system, prevents cancer, good to fight constipation (Fibre-rich), dissolves stagnation.
Cooking time approx. 20 min
Allergens: AG
4 portions to 116,25g. / 94kcal. - (carb:55% / prot:45%)
100g.=80,86kcal. / protein 2,68g. fat:2,83g.
µg. - Ph:4,15 Na:4,56 Ka:16,7 Mg:1,23 Ca:1,78 Fe:0,06 Zn:0,03 Col.:0,25 Hsr.:1,27

**Quantity of ingredients:**
Potato (mealy) 5/8 oz / 200g. (yes)
Carrot 1 piece / 50g. (yes)
Sour cream 15% fat 3 table spoons / 45g. (little)
Onion (spring onion) 1 piece / 20g. (yes)
Rucola 1/2 bunch / 100g. ()
Lemon peel 1/4 teaspoon / 1g. (yes)
Salt 1 pinch / 1g. (little)
Pepper (ground) 1 pinch / 0,2g. ()
Whole grain bread 8 slices / 48g. (yes)

**Cooking instructions:**
Cook the potatoes gently, peel and squeeze through the potato press.
Cook vegetable broth according to the basic recipe and remove a carrot
after a short cooking time and finely crush with a fork.
Stir the potatoes, carrots, grated lemon zest and sour cream into a
smooth cream.
Mix carrot and potato cream with finely chopped rocket salad. Season
the spread with salt and pepper and spread the bread. Sprinkle with the
finely chopped young onions.

## 9.19 Chicken soup with egg yolk and parsley

Strengthens blood, strengthens bone marrow, reduces blood pressure,
strengthens immune system. Parsley stimulates liver function,
harmonizes liver and spleen, strengthens eyesight, detoxifying.
Cooking time approx. 10 min
Allergens: CL
2 portions to 260g. / 118kcal. - (carb:82% / prot:18%)
100g.=45,19kcal. / protein 16,35g. fat:2,49g.
µg. - Ph:6,98 Na:8,83 Ka:9 Mg:24,79 Ca:69,4 Fe:0,28 Zn:0,05 Col.:6,52 Hsr.:2,22

**Quantity of ingredients:**
Basic recipe for a chicken soup (warming) 2 cup / 500g. (yes)
Chicken yolk 1 piece / 10g. (yes)
Parsley 1 table spoon / 10g. (yes)

**Cooking instructions:**
Cook the chicken broth according to the basic recipe.
Heat broth and bubble the egg yolk. Sprinkle the chopped parsley over
it and let it rest for about 2 minutes. Drink in small sips.

## 9.20 Coffee

Supports urination, stimulates appetite, detoxifying, increases blood
glucose levels, harmonizes heart rhythm.
Cooking time approx. 5 min
1 portion to 129g. / 16kcal. - (carb:100% / prot:0%)
100g.=12,4kcal. / protein 0,01g. fat:0g.
µg. - Ph:0,08 Na:0,97 Ka:2,62 Mg:1,16 Ca:4,76 Fe:0,02 Zn:0,09 Col.:0 Hsr.:3,91

**Quantity of ingredients:**
Coffee 1 table spoon / 5g. (yes)
Water 1 cup / 120g. (yes)
Sugar white 1 teaspoon / 4g. (little)

**Cooking instructions:**
Depending on your taste, prepare a filter coffee, espresso or "Turkish".

## 9.21 Colorful rice dish

Strengthens immune system, good to fight diabetes, strengthens spleen and stomach, strengthens blood, strengthens the muscles, tendons and bones, promotes digestion, helps to digest fat, supports urination, reduces blood pressure, dissolves stagnation.
Cooking time approx. 45 min
Allergens: L
3 portions to 342,67g. / 437kcal. - (carb:63% / prot:37%)
100g.=127,63kcal. / protein 17,03g. fat:10,23g.
µg. - Ph:7,97 Na:4,89 Ka:17,25 Mg:6,38 Ca:18,08 Fe:0,14 Zn:0,11 Col.:1 Hsr.:5,14

**Quantity of ingredients:**
Olive oil 2 teaspoons / 20g. (yes)
Onion (spring onion) 1 piece / 20g. (yes)
Beef meat 1/4 lbs - 4oz / 125g. (yes)
Rice (whole grain) 3 oz / 80g. (yes)
Basic recipe for a vegetable soup (nutritious) 1 cup / 300g. (yes)
Celery root 1/8 lbs - 2oz / 50g. (yes)
Leek 1 piece / 100g. (yes)
Beans (green, fresh) 3/8 lbs - 6oz / 150g. (yes)
Carrot 1 piece / 70g. (yes)
Tomato 2 pieces / 100g. (yes)
Salt 1 pinch / 0,5g. (little)
Pepper (ground) 1 pinch / 0,2g. ()
Peppers powder 1 pinch / 0,5g. (yes)
Herbs various 2 table spoons / 12g. (yes)

**Cooking instructions:**
Wash leek and carrots, clean and chop them. Dice the celery, slice the tomatoes.
Fry in a large, deep pan with oil, onion and minced meat.
Add brown rice and prepared vegetables (celery, leeks, beans, carrots, tomatoes). Braise briefly.
Season with salt, pepper and paprika. Add vegetable broth. Heat till it boils and cook over low heat for 20 to 30 minutes with the lid closed.
Sprinkle with fresh chopped herbs and serve.

## 9.22 Colorful Tuscan bean soup

Promotes digestion, helps to digest fat, supports urination, reduces blood pressure, diuretic, calms the stomach.
Cooking time approx. 2 hours
Allergens: L
3 portions to 256g. / 249kcal. - (carb:38% / prot:62%)
100g.=97,27kcal. / protein 6,91g. fat:17,64g.
µg. - Ph:1,92 Na:0,64 Ka:6,57 Mg:1,02 Ca:1,91 Fe:0,4 Zn:0,03 Col.:0,01 Hsr.:3,71

**Quantity of ingredients:**
Kidney beans (red) 1/8 lbs - 2oz / 50g. (yes)
Chickpeas 1 oz / 25g. (yes)
Lentils 1 oz / 25g. (yes)
Celery sticks 1 stick / 10g. (yes)
Tomato 2 pieces / 100g. (yes)
Fennel seeds ground 1/2 teaspoon / 1g. (yes)
Salt 1 pinch / 1g. (little)
Pepper (ground) 1 pinch / 0,5g. ()
Garlic 1 clove / 3g. (yes)
Olive oil 3 table spoons / 50g. (yes)
Water 2 1/4 cups / 500g. (yes)
Basil (fresh) 5-7 leaves / 3g. (yes)

**Cooking instructions:**
Soak legumes, boil and puree. Add vegetables, spices, herbs and oil and cook gently for 2 hours.

Variation: Sweet chestnuts give the dish a special Italian touch.


## 9.23 Compote from plums

Cancer preventive effect, dehydrates the body, stimulates digestion and binds fats in the intestine.
Cooking time approx. 10 min
2 portions to 170,5g. / 22kcal. - (carb:93% / prot:7%)
100g.=13,2kcal. / protein 0,32g. fat:0,06g.
µg. - Ph:1,73 Na:0,34 Ka:17,94 Mg:0,8 Ca:2,7 Fe:0,03 Zn:0,02 Col.:0 Hsr.:1,47

**Quantity of ingredients:**
Plums 1/4 lbs - 4oz / 100g. (yes)
Water 1 1/2 cups / 240g. (yes)
Cinnamon ground 1 pinch / 1g. (yes)

**Cooking instructions:**
Boil plums in water until soft. Sprinkle with a little cinnamon.

## 9.24 Compote from rhubarb

Antipyretic, analgesic, detoxifying, bactericide.
Cooking time approx. 15 min
1 portion to 230g. / 48kcal. - (carb:92% / prot:8%)
100g.=20,87kcal. / protein 0,64g. fat:0,1g.
µg. - Ph:11,22 Na:1,7 Ka:119,43 Mg:6,43 Ca:25,43 Fe:0,28 Zn:0,15 Col.:0 Hsr.:2,61

**Quantity of ingredients:**
Rhubarb 1/4 lbs - 4oz / 100g. (yes)
Water 1 cup / 120g. (yes)
Honey 1 table spoon / 10g. (little)

**Cooking instructions:**
Wash rhubarb and cut small. Boil in the water. Allow to cool a little and add the honey.

## 9.25 Cottage cheese with steamed fruit

Good to fight loss of appetite, promotes digestion, supports urination.
Cooking time approx. 20 min
Allergens: G
2 portions to 250g. / 214kcal. - (carb:40% / prot:60%)
100g.=85,8kcal. / protein 18,45g. fat:6,4g.
µg. - Ph:22,3 Na:57,25 Ka:25,45 Mg:1,85 Ca:12,8 Fe:0,05 Zn:0,09 Col.:0,64 Hsr.:1,5

**Quantity of ingredients:**
Cottage cheese 3/4 lbs / 300g. (yes)
Apple (sour) 1 piece / 100g. (yes)
Pear 1 piece / 100g. (yes)

**Cooking instructions:**
Wash apples and pears well, do not peel, and chop small. In a pot with steam filter, boil them al dente, remove and allow to cool down.
Serve the cheese, spread the fruit on it.

## 9.26 Cranberry juice

Antibacterial, good to fight loss of appetite, arteriosclerosis, bladder infections, diarrhea, colds. Antipyretic, against free radicals, gout, diuretic, stomach ulcers, oral mucosa inflammation, rheumatism.
Cooking time approx. 5 min
1 portion to 160g. / 43kcal. - (carb:98% / prot:2%)
100g.=26,88kcal. / protein 0,14g. fat:0,02g.
µg. - Ph:2,06 Na:1,53 Ka:11,69 Mg:1,16 Ca:4,22 Fe:0,09 Zn:0,09 Col.:0 Hsr.:3,12

**Quantity of ingredients:**
Cranberries 2 table spoons / 25g. (yes)
Water 1 cup / 125g. (yes)
Honey 1 table spoon / 10g. (little)

**Cooking instructions:**
Mix the cranberries with a little water with the blender to a pulp. Add the remaining water and sweeten with the honey.

## 9.27 Cucumber soup

Diuretic, detoxifying, suppresses conversion of sugar into fat, lowers cholesterol, prevents cancer, promotes digestion, diaphoretic, dries out, good to fight yeast infections.
Cooking time approx. 20 min
Allergens: M
4 portions to 235,25g. / 96kcal. - (carb:22% / prot:78%)
100g.=40,6kcal. / protein 0,91g. fat:9,03g.
µg. - Ph:2,67 Na:1,28 Ka:15,6 Mg:1,17 Ca:2,57 Fe:0,06 Zn:0,01 Col.:0 Hsr.:0,85

**Quantity of ingredients:**
Olive oil 2 table spoons / 35g. (yes)
Cucumber 2 pieces / 400g. (yes)
Water 2 cup / 500g. (yes)
Sage 3 leaves / 3g. (yes)
Mustard 1/2 teaspoon / 0,5g. (yes)
Coriander 1 pinch / 1g. (yes)
Cardamom 1 pinch / 1g. (yes)
Salt 1 pinch / 1g. (little)

**Cooking instructions:**
Heat oil and roast short the small cucumbers. Add Mustard seeds, coriander, cardamom and salt. Add water. Simmer for 10-15 min. Puree and decorate with fresh chopped sage.

## 9.28 Curdcheesedumplings on strawberry pulp

Strawberry forcing spleen and stomach, strengthens blood. Chicken egg calms nerves and stomach.
Cooking time approx. 30 min
Allergens: ACG
5 portions to 296,2g. / 553kcal. - (carb:40% / prot:60%)
100g.=186,77kcal. / protein 18,89g. fat:46,85g.
µg. - Ph:5,33 Na:3,67 Ka:5,89 Mg:0,95 Ca:2,43 Fe:0,04 Zn:0,02 Col.:2,41 Hsr.:0,72

**Quantity of ingredients:**
Curd cheese 20% 1,1 lbs / 500g. (yes)
Spelled semolina 3/8 lbs - 6oz / 150g. (yes)
Butter organic 1/8 lbs - 2oz / 40g. (little)
Chicken egg 2 pieces / 120g. (yes)
Sugar - icing sugar 2 table spoons / 20g. (little)
Salt 1 pinch / 1g. (little)
Breadcrumbs (wheat bread, bread roll) 3 table spoons / 25g. (yes)
Butter organic 1/4 lbs - 4oz / 100g. (little)
Strawberries 1,1 lbs / 500g. (yes)
Sugar - icing sugar 3 table spoons / 25g. (little)

**Cooking instructions:**
Curd-cheese, grit, butter, eggs, powdered sugar and salt to a smooth dough. Keep the dough 15 mins in the refrigerator to settle down. Then shape small dumplings with a diameter of approx. 4cm and boil them for about 10 minutes in slightly boiling salt water. Heat butter in a pan and roast the breadcrumbs golden brown. Roll the dumplings carefully into the crumbs.
Serve the dumplings with the strawberry.

## 9.29 Delicately spiced zucchini with tomatoes

Diuretic, promotes digestion, helps to digest fat, reduces blood pressure, dissolves stagnation, antioxidative, supports urination, diuretic, warming the body from the inside, expands blood vessels.
Cooking time approx. 10 min
4 portions to 396,5g. / 203kcal. - (carb:72% / prot:28%)
100g.=51,2kcal. / protein 5,38g. fat:6,62g.
µg. - Ph:10,4 Na:0,79 Ka:35,33 Mg:6,3 Ca:5,58 Fe:0,26 Zn:0,02 Col.:0 Hsr.:5,53

**Quantity of ingredients:**
Olive oil 1 table spoon / 20g. (yes)
Onion white 2 pieces / 120g. (yes)
Zucchini 4 pieces / 800g. (yes)
Oregano dried 1 pinch / 1g. (yes)
Basil (fresh) 6-8 leaves / 3g. (yes)
Salt 1 pinch / 1g. (little)
Tomato 2 pieces / 120g. (yes)
Rice (whole grain) 1 cup / 120g. (yes)
Water 6 cups / 400g. (yes)
Salt 1 pinch / 1g. (little)

**Cooking instructions:**
In a hot pan, fry olive oil, finely chopped onions and finely chopped zucchini until half cooked. Add plenty of dried oregano. Salt and chop the tomatoes for a few minutes until the zucchini are tender but crisp. Add fresh basil as desired.
Variation: Put some sheep's cheese over the tomatoes and finish cooking with the lid closed.
Place the rice in salted water, heat till it boils and let it simmer over low heat for about 15 minutes.

## 9.30 Fast polenta with avocado and spring onion

Good to fight inflammations, swelling, pain. Forcing spleen and stomach, lets urine and bile juice flow, dissolves stagnation. Includes unsaturated fatty acids, antioxidative.
Cooking time approx. 10 min
2 portions to 286g. / 450kcal. - (carb:55% / prot:45%)
100g.=157,17kcal. / protein 6,92g. fat:27,5g.
µg. - Ph:16,92 Na:0,99 Ka:54,42 Mg:8,7 Ca:3,02 Fe:0,13 Zn:0,17 Col.:0,01 Hsr.:3,78

**Quantity of ingredients:**
Corn (fast polenta) 1 cup / 120g. (yes)
Water 1 1/2 cups / 240g. (yes)
Olive oil 1 table spoon / 15g. (yes)
Salt 1 pinch / 1g. (little)
Pepper (ground) 1 pinch / 0,5g. ()
Lemon juice 1 dash / 3g. (yes)
Onion (spring onion) 2 pieces / 40g. (yes)
Avocado 1/2 piece / 150g. (little)
Turmeric (yellow root) 1 pinch / 1g. (yes)
Basil (fresh) 1 teaspoon / 2g. (yes)

**Cooking instructions:**
Heat water, add oil, lemon and spices.
When the water boils, add the polenta while stirring constantly and cook for 2 minutes.
When the porridge becomes firm, the polenta is ready.
Add diced avocado and sliced spring onion to the polenta. Sprinkle fresh basil on it.

## 9.31 Fennel and potato gratin

Reduces inflammation, improves blood circulation, improves digestion, supports urination, lowers cholesterol, good to fight loss of appetite, flatulence, inflammatory bowel disease, heartburn. Forcing spleen, improves blood circulation.
Cooking time approx. 1 1/2 hours
Allergens: CGL
2 portions to 230,5g. / 147kcal. - (carb:68% / prot:32%)
100g.=63,77kcal. / protein 5,72g. fat:5,42g.
µg. - Ph:15 Na:12,98 Ka:80,91 Mg:13,52 Ca:40,41 Fe:0,41 Zn:0,09 Col.:7,81 Hsr.:3,64

**Quantity of ingredients:**
Fennel 5/8 oz / 200g. (yes)
Potato 1/4 lbs - 4oz / 125g. (yes)
Basic recipe for a vegetable soup (nutritious) 1/2 cup / 100g. (yes)
Butter organic 1 teaspoon / 3g. (little)
Rice flour 2 teaspoons / 6g. (yes)
Cream sour 10% 1 teaspoon / 3g. (yes)
Salt 1 pinch / 1g. (little)
Sugar cane sugar 1 pinch / 1g. (little)
Chicken yolk 1 piece / 10g. (yes)
Pepper Cayenne 1 pinch / 0,5g. (yes)
Nutmeg 1 pinch / 0,5g. (yes)
Parsley 1 teaspoon / 2g. (yes)
Chives 1 teaspoon / 3g. (yes)
Parmesan 1 teaspoon / 3g. (little)
Butter organic 1 teaspoon / 3g. (little)

**Cooking instructions:**
Cook peeled potatoes and then let cool. Wash the fennel, cut off the stems and remove any outer leaves.
Hold back fennel greens and add it to the sauce with the other herbs later.
Steam the fennel tubers for about 15 - 20 minutes.
Then cut the potatoes and fennel into slices and place in layers in a

greased baking dish.
Bring the liquid of fennel broth to the boil and bind it with flour.
Season with sea salt, cayenne pepper, sugar, nutmeg and sour cream.
Allow to cool and alloy with egg yolk.
Spread the sauce over the casserole, sprinkle with parmesan and finely chopped parsley and chives. Bake at 200 °C / 392 °F in the oven for half an hour.

## 9.32 Fennel-Rice Soup

Forcing spleen, relieves constipation, stimulates nerves, detoxifying, reduces inflammation, improves blood circulation.
Cooking time approx. 15-20 min
Allergens: EG
2 portions to 234g. / 156kcal. - (carb:88% / prot:12%)
100g.=66,45kcal. / protein 3,57g. fat:6,64g.
µg. - Ph:7,34 Na:16,24 Ka:41,07 Mg:52,9 Ca:55,34 Fe:0,27 Zn:0,06 Col.:1,92 Hsr.:2,45

**Quantity of ingredients:**
Basic recipe for a rice soup (Congee) 1 cup / 300g. (yes)
Fennel 1/2 piece / 150g. (yes)
Butter organic 1 table spoon / 15g. (little)
Soy sauce 1 dash / 3g. (yes)

**Cooking instructions:**
Cook the fennel softly in the rice soup according to the basic recipe.
Before serving, add a piece of butter and some soy sauce.

## 9.33 Fruit juice

Stops diarrhea, promotes digestion, appetizing, harmonizes the stomach, relieves pain, detoxifying, reduces blood pressure, strengthens immune system, prevents cancer, reduces radiation damage.
Cooking time approx. 10 min
2 portions to 305g. / 176kcal. - (carb:93% / prot:7%)
100g.=57,54kcal. / protein 1,89g. fat:0,9g.
µg. - Ph:4,99 Na:2,24 Ka:37,45 Mg:2,36 Ca:6,04 Fe:0,21 Zn:0,05 Col.:0 Hsr.:4,3

**Quantity of ingredients:**
Orange 2 pieces / 150g. (yes)
Apple (sweet) 4 pieces / 300g. (yes)
Carrot 2 pieces / 150g. (yes)
Honey 1 table spoon / 10g. (little)

**Cooking instructions:**
Peel oranges and carrots. Cut all ingredients into cubes so that they fit into the juicer and juice. Sweet with honey.

## 9.34 Grated carrots with apple

Promotes spleen and liver, reduces blood pressure, strengthens immune system, prevents cancer, reduces radiation damage, stops diarrhea, promotes digestion, appetizing, harmonizes the stomach.
Cooking time approx. 10 min
1 portion to 154g. / 74kcal. - (carb:91% / prot:9%)
100g.=48,05kcal. / protein 1,21g. fat:0,41g.
µg. - Ph:26,57 Na:19,84 Ka:140,47 Mg:10,21 Ca:29,74 Fe:1,4 Zn:0,36 Col.:0 Hsr.:18,25

**Quantity of ingredients:**
Carrot 1/4 lbs - 4oz / 100g. (yes)
Apple (sweet) 1 piece / 50g. (yes)
Lemon juice 2 teaspoons / 3g. (yes)
Sugar substitute (sweetener) 1g. Or 0,034oz / 1g. (yes)

**Cooking instructions:**
Mix lemon juice with sweetener. Grate the washed, thinly peeled carrots and the apple piece into the sauce and mix.

## 9.35 Grilled tomatoes with cheese filling

Promotes digestion, helps to digest fat, supports urination, reduces blood pressure, stimulates digestion.
Cooking time approx. 30 min
Allergens: ACG
2 portions to 319,5g. / 470kcal. - (carb:38% / prot:62%)
100g.=146,95kcal. / protein 18,89g. fat:30,98g.
µg. - Ph:25,05 Na:101,57 Ka:41,33 Mg:3,14 Ca:21,11 Fe:0,17 Zn:0,12 Col.:13,64
Hsr.:4,36

**Quantity of ingredients:**
Tomato 8 pieces / 200g. (yes)
Feta cheese 0,2 lbs / 75g. (yes)
Fresh cheese 0,2 lbs / 75g. (yes)
Chicken egg 1 piece / 60g. (yes)
Olive oil 1 table spoon / 12g. (yes)

Basil (fresh) 1 table spoon / 6g. (yes)
Salt 1 pinch / 1g. (little)
Pepper (ground) 1 pinch / 0,5g. ()
Olives 1 oz / 30g. (yes)
Rucola 1/4 lbs / 100g. ()
White bread (wheat bread) 4 slices / 80g. (little)

**Cooking instructions:**
Hollow out tomatoes generously. Put in a casserole dish.
Mix cheese, olive oil, egg, chopped basil and flour. Season with salt and pepper and fill in the tomatoes.
Bake in the preheated oven at 210 degrees on the middle rail for 15 minutes, then switch on the oven grill and grill for a further 3 minutes (without circulating air).
Stone the olives and chop and sprinkle on the tomatoes.
Garnish tomatoes with rocket and serve with white bread.

# 9.36 Hearty polenta mash

Strengths spleen and stomach, promotes watering, promotes digestion, detoxifying, promotes perspiration, reduces blood lipids, stimulates, dissolves stagnation, stimulates appetite, dissolves stagnation.
Cooking time approx. 10 min
2 portions to 207,5g. / 262kcal. - (carb:80% / prot:20%)
100g.=126,27kcal. / protein 5,65g. fat:5,94g.
µg. - Ph:6,71 Na:0,73 Ka:11,2 Mg:2,2 Ca:2,17 Fe:0,09 Zn:0,05 Col.:0 Hsr.:2,46

**Quantity of ingredients:**
Corn Grease (Polenta) 1 cup / 120g. (yes)
Onion (spring onion) 2 pieces / 40g. (yes)
Ginger fresh 1/2 teaspoon / 2g. (yes)
Nutmeg 1 pinch / 1g. (yes)
Salt 1 pinch / 1g. (little)
Olive oil 1 table spoon / 10g. (yes)
Turmeric (yellow root) 1 pinch / 1g. (yes)
Water 1 1/2 cups / 240g. (yes)

**Cooking instructions:**
Stir in the polenta in boiling water and let it swell for 7 min. Add green onion, grated ginger, turmeric, nutmeg, salt and olive oil and wait for 3 more minutes.

## 9.37 Kohlrabi in chervil sauce with potatoes

Reduces inflammation, lowers cholesterol, diuretic, conducts bowel winds, strengthens immune system, prevents cancer, promotes weight loss. Good to fight loss of appetite, flatulence, high blood pressure, depressions, diabetes, diarrhea.
Cooking time approx. 1 hour
Allergens: GL
4 portions to 316,75g. / 188kcal. - (carb:79% / prot:21%)
100g.=59,19kcal. / protein 8,66g. fat:2,51g.
µg. - Ph:2,95 Na:1,03 Ka:25,06 Mg:3,48 Ca:15,16 Fe:0,04 Zn:0,02 Col.:0,06 Hsr.:0,91

**Quantity of ingredients:**
Potato 6 pieces / 450g. (yes)
Basic recipe for a vegetable soup (nutritious) 1 cup / 300g. (yes)
Potato 1/4 lbs - 4oz / 100g. (yes)
Nutmeg 1 pinch / 0,2g. (yes)
Lemon peel 1/2 teaspoon / 2g. (yes)
Ginger fresh 1/2 teaspoon / 2g. (yes)
Lovage 1/2 teaspoon / 2g. (yes)
Kohlrabi 3/4 lbs / 300g. (yes)
Salt 1 pinch / 1g. (little)
Pepper (ground) 1 pinch / 0,2g. ()
Sour cream 15% fat 3 table spoons / 30g. (little)
Chervil dried 1 Bunch / 80g. (yes)

**Cooking instructions:**
Boil the potatoes in salted water.
Bring half of the vegetable stock to boil. Add the diced potatoes, nutmeg, lemon zest, ginger and lovage. Cover the potatoes and cook for about 10 minutes until soft and puree them with a blender until they are smooth.
Bring remaining vegetable stock to boil. Cut kohlrabi into cubes and add, cover and cook for about 8 minutes. Stir in the potato sauce and heat everything briefly.
Puree with the mixing stick chervil and sour cream. Mix the chervil cream with the kohlrabi vegetables.
Serve with the cooked, peeled potatoes.

## 9.38 Leek and potato gratin

Reduces inflammation, improves digestion, regenerates skin, supports urination, lowers cholesterol, promotes sweating, dissolves stagnation.
Cooking time approx. 1 hour
Allergens: CGL
4 portions to 346,5g. / 368kcal. - (carb:56% / prot:44%)
100g.=106,35kcal. / protein 7,73g. fat:16,47g.
µg. - Ph:3,43 Na:5,61 Ka:14,59 Mg:1,08 Ca:3,84 Fe:0,04 Zn:0,03 Col.:1,24 Hsr.:1,42

**Quantity of ingredients:**
Potato 1,1 lbs / 500g. (yes)
Leek 1,1 lbs / 500g. (yes)
Apple (sour) 1 piece / 200g. (yes)
Crème fraiche cheese 1/4 lbs - 4oz / 125g. (little)
Basic recipe for a vegetable soup (nutritious) 1/4 cup / 20g. (yes)
Chicken yolk 1 piece / 20g. (yes)
Emmental cheese 2 table spoons / 20g. (yes)
Salt 1 pinch / 1g. (little)
Pepper (ground) 1 pinch / 0,5g. ()

**Cooking instructions:**
Wash the potatoes, peel, cut into very thin slices and pat dry. Place half in a flat greased baking dish.
Clean and wash leeks and cut into fine rings. Wash apple, peel and cut into thin slices. Spread the leek rings and apple slices on top. Put the remaining potato slices on top.
Mix crème fraîche, egg yolk, grated Emmentaler, salt and pepper, if necessary add some vegetable stock and pour over the casserole.
Bake at 200°C/392°F in the oven for about 45 to 50 minutes until golden brown. Cover with parchment paper after 30 minutes to prevent the burr from drying out.

## 9.39 Lettuce with vinegar dressing

Relieves fatigue, regulates gastrointestinal function, dissolves stagnation, laxative, antiparasitic, improves blood circulation, detoxifying, reduces inflammation, relieves pain.
Cooking time approx. 10 min
Allergens: O
2 portions to 127,5g. / 68kcal. - (carb:32% / prot:68%)
100g.=52,94kcal. / protein 1,64g. fat:4,88g.
µg. - Ph:8,07 Na:2,56 Ka:49,71 Mg:2,9 Ca:8,86 Fe:0,22 Zn:0,09 Col.:0 Hsr.:5

**Quantity of ingredients:**
Lettuce 1 piece / 200g. (rec.)
Vinegar (Apple vinegar) 1 table spoon / 10g. (yes)
Water 1 table spoon / 10g. (yes)
Rapeseed oil 1 table spoon / 10g. (yes)
Onion (spring onion) 1 piece / 20g. (yes)
Salt 1 pinch / 0,5g. (little)
Pepper (ground) 1 pinch / 0,1g. ()
Chives 1 table spoon / 5g. (yes)

**Cooking instructions:**
Clean lettuce, wash and drain. Add the ingredients to the marinade in an extra container. Salad with marinade just before consumption. Just before, sprinkle with chives.

## 9.40 Melanzani with olive oil and turmeric

improves blood circulation, reduces inflammation, relieves pain, promotes digestion, helps to digest fat, supports urination, reduces blood pressure.
Cooking time approx. 30 min
Allergens: A
2 portions to 321,5g. / 432kcal. - (carb:47% / prot:53%)
100g.=134,37kcal. / protein 6,13g. fat:30,66g.
µg. - Ph:6,14 Na:10,38 Ka:42,8 Mg:2,74 Ca:3,55 Fe:0,09 Zn:0,05 Col.:0,02 Hsr.:4,84

**Quantity of ingredients:**
Aubergine 2 pieces / 300g. (yes)
Olive oil 4 table spoons / 60g. (yes)
Tomato 4 pieces / 200g. (yes)
Turmeric (yellow root) 1/2 teaspoon / 1g. (yes)
Ground 1 pinch / 1g. (yes)
Salt 1 pinch / 1g. (little)
White bread (wheat bread) 4 slices / 80g. (little)

**Cooking instructions:**
Cut the Melanzani into slices and spread them with the tomatoes on a baking tray. Sprinkle with olive oil and then with turmeric, caraway and salt. Bake them in the tube 20 min.
Serve with the white bread.

## 9.41 Millet with pears

Refreshing and nourishing, promotes digestion, supports urination, good to fight cough, promotes perspiration, reduces blood lipids, stimulates, dissolves stagnation, forces liver, strengthens the muscles, lowers cholesterol, antiparasitic.
Cooking time approx. 35 min
Allergens: G
5 portions to 238,4g. / 213kcal. - (carb:86% / prot:14%)
100g.=89,43kcal. / protein 3,91g. fat:3,24g.
µg. - Ph:1,89 Na:0,11 Ka:4,29 Mg:0,99 Ca:0,53 Fe:0,05 Zn:0,02 Col.:0 Hsr.:0,77

**Quantity of ingredients:**
Millet 1 cup / 120g. (yes)
Water 1 1/2 cups / 200g. (yes)
Grape juice red 1 1/2 cups / 240g. (yes)
Pear 4 pieces / 600g. (yes)
Ginger fresh 1/2 teaspoon / 2g. (yes)
Salt 1 pinch / 1g. (little)
Acerola fruit nectar or powder 1 teaspoon / 2g. (little)
Cocoa 1 pinch / 1g. (yes)
Sunflower seeds 2 table spoons / 4g. (yes)
Barley malt 1/2 teaspoon / 2g. (yes)
Cream, sweet 30% 2 teaspoons / 20g. (little)

**Cooking instructions:**
Simmer the millet for 5 min and let it swell for another 30 min.

Then: In a hot pot, heat some grape juice; add chopped pears, very little grated ginger, a pinch of salt, acerola, a pinch of cocoa and sauté briefly; add the boiled millet, sunflower seeds, some barley malt to taste, 1 tsp cream per
serving or a little butter.

## 9.42 Miso soup with tofu

Vitamins, minerals and secondary plant active ingredients, invigorating, detoxifying, strengthens immune system, promotes digestion, forcing spleen, containing enzymes, reduces flatulence, alginic acid detoxifies the bowel, dissolves stagnation.
Cooking time approx. 5 min
Allergens: E
3 portions to 231,33g. / 51kcal. - (carb:43% / prot:57%)
100g.=22,05kcal. / protein 4,43g. fat:1,66g.
µg. - Ph:3,77 Na:19,37 Ka:6,35 Mg:1,96 Ca:2,38 Fe:0,02 Zn:0,01 Col.:0 Hsr.:1,11

**Quantity of ingredients:**
Wakame 1 piece / 5g. (yes)
Miso 3-4 table spoons / 30g. (yes)
Soy Tofu 1/8 lbs - 2oz / 50g. (yes)
Water 2 cup / 500g. (yes)
Soy sauce 1 dash / 3g. (yes)
Onion (spring onion) 1/2 teaspoon / 6g. (yes)

**Cooking instructions:**
Boil soybean seedlings, wakame algae and diced tofu for 5 minutes.
Put the miso paste in the soup plate and slowly pour over the soup.
Season with Tamari sauce. Sprinkle with cutted spring onion.

## 9.43 Oat Congee

Strengthens immune system.
Cooking time approx. 2-4 hours
Allergens: A
3 portions to 275g. / 162kcal. - (carb:74% / prot:26%)
100g.=58,91kcal. / protein 7,04g. fat:2,87g.
µg. - Ph:5,76 Na:0,23 Ka:5,98 Mg:2,27 Ca:1,82 Fe:0,1 Zn:0,08 Col.:0 Hsr.:2,51

**Quantity of ingredients:**
Oat 1 cup / 125g. (yes)
Water 6 cups / 700g. (yes)

**Cooking instructions:**
Cook oats and water in a ratio of about 1: 6. The amount of water
determines the thickness of the mash (pure matter of taste). The oats
swell, so do not take much. Put the oats in a saucepan with good
insulation and a heavy lid. It is important to simmer the oats after a
short boil on the slightest flame, otherwise it burns. Cook the oat for 2-4
hours. The longer it cooks, the more he strengthens.

## 9.44 Oatmeal soup with spring onion and carrots

Reduces blood pressure, strengthens immune system, prevents cancer,
reduces radiation damage, stimulates digestion, reduces pain,
stimulates appetite, dissolves stagnation.
Cooking time approx. 30 min
Allergens: AG
3 portions to 266,33g. / 135kcal. - (carb:65% / prot:35%)
100g.=50,56kcal. / protein 3,87g. fat:5,59g.
µg. - Ph:3,67 Na:1,03 Ka:7,89 Mg:1,41 Ca:2,55 Fe:0,1 Zn:0,05 Col.:0,5 Hsr.:1,63

**Quantity of ingredients:**
Oat 6 table spoons / 48g. (yes)
Carrot 2 pieces / 200g. (yes)
Butter organic 1 table spoon / 15g. (little)
Nutmeg 1 pinch / 1g. (yes)
Lovage 1 stem / 15g. (yes)
Onion (spring onion) 2 pieces / 40g. (yes)
Water 2 cup / 480g. (yes)

**Cooking instructions:**
Roast the oats in butter, add salt and spices, pour in water and heat till it boils. After 10 min. add the grated carrots
and lovage, cook for 10 minutes. Finely add chopped onion.

## 9.45 Oven potatoes with celery-curd cheese (quark)

Promotes spleen, reduces Inflammation, improves digestion, regenerates skin, supports urination, lowers cholesterol.
Cooking time approx. 30 min
Allergens: GL
2 portions to 398g. / 304kcal. - (carb:52% / prot:48%)
100g.=76,38kcal. / protein 15,61g. fat:24,04g.
µg. - Ph:19,06 Na:6,87 Ka:59,91 Mg:7,16 Ca:24,85 Fe:0,1 Zn:0,08 Col.:1,01 Hsr.:3,76

**Quantity of ingredients:**
Celery root 3 oz / 80g. (yes)
Basic recipe for a vegetable soup (nutritious) 1/2 cup / 100g. (yes)
Ground caraway 1 pinch / 0,2g. (yes)
Lemon peel 1/2 teaspoon / 1g. (yes)
Salt 1 pinch / 1g. (little)
Pepper (ground) 1 pinch / 0,2g. ()
Lemon juice 1 teaspoon / 3g. (yes)
Curd cheese 20% 5/8 oz / 200g. (yes)
Crème fraiche cheese 1/2 teaspoon / 5g. (little)
Potato 6 pieces / 400g. (yes)
Olive oil 2 teaspoons / 5g. (yes)
Salt 1 pinch / 1g. (little)

**Cooking instructions:**
Celery-curd cheese:
Mix celery with vegetable broth according to basic recipe, caraway and lemon peel. Cook for about 8 minutes until the celery is soft and the vegetable broth almost evaporated. Mix the celery vegetable broth with

the lemon juice, finely, and stir until smooth. Season with salt and pepper.

Baked potatoes:
Preheat oven to 200 °C / 400 °F.
Brush the potatoes well, halve them, and place them on a baking tray with the cut surface facing up. Lightly salt the surfaces and sprinkle with oil. Fry the potatoes in the oven for about 25 minutes.
Serve the celery plug to the potatoes.

## 9.46 Pancakes with spinach and parmesan

Promotes bowel movement, improves blood circulation, forcing spleen and bowel, strengthens immune system, good to fight loss of appetite, flatulence, high blood pressure, depressions, diabetes, constipation, inflammatory bowel disease
Cooking time approx. 25 min
Allergens: ACGL
6 portions to 303g. / 330kcal. - (carb:46% / prot:54%)
100g.=108,8kcal. / protein 17,5g. fat:18,52g.
µg. - Ph:3,27 Na:3,24 Ka:6,47 Mg:0,96 Ca:4,52 Fe:0,05 Zn:0,02 Col.:1,32 Hsr.:1,02

**Quantity of ingredients:**
Wholemeal flour 1/4 lbs - 4oz / 100g. (yes)
Wheat flour 1/4 lbs - 4oz / 100g. (yes)
Chicken egg 4 pieces / 200g. (yes)
Cow's milk (whole milk 3.5% fat) 1 1/2 cups / 400g. (yes)
Salt 1 pinch / 1g. (little)
Sunflower oil 1 table spoon / 15g. (yes)
Olive oil 1 table spoon / 15g. (yes)
Onion white 1 piece / 50g. (yes)
Parsley 1/2 bunch / 80g. (yes)
Basic recipe for a vegetable soup (nutritious) 1/2 cup / 150g. (yes)
Basil (fresh) 1/4 teaspoon / 1g. (yes)
Nutmeg 1 pinch / 0,3g. (yes)
Crème fraiche cheese 3 table spoons / 45g. (little)
Spinach 1,3 lbs / 600g. (yes)
Salt 1 pinch / 1g. (little)
Pepper (ground) 1 pinch / 0,1g. ()
Parmesan 1/8 lbs - 2oz / 60g. (little)

**Cooking instructions:**
Stir flour, eggs and milk and a pinch of salt with the whisk until smooth.
From the dough, fry pancakes crispy brown on both sides.

Heat oil in a small saucepan. Fry the finely chopped onion until tender.
Stir in chopped parsley, sauté briefly. Add the vegetable broth
according to the basic recipe, season with basil and nutmeg. Cover and
simmer for 15 minutes,
add creme fraiche and finely puree.
Cook the washed, drizzled spinach with a little salt in a closed pan over
a moderate heat in 3 minutes, drain in a sieve and cut into small pieces.
Add the spinach to the sauce, heat briefly. Add parmesan in the mix.
Fill the pancakes with the cream spinach.


# 9.47 Pear juice

Promotes digestion, supports urination.
Cooking time approx. 5 min
2 portions to 300g. / 180kcal. - (carb:93% / prot:7%)
100g.=60kcal. / protein 1,8g. fat:1,2g.
µg. - Ph:7,5 Na:1 Ka:62,5 Mg:3,5 Ca:4,5 Fe:0,15 Zn:0,05 Col.:0 Hsr.:7,5

**Quantity of ingredients:**
Pear 3 pieces / 600g. (yes)

**Cooking instructions:**
Peel pears thinly (vitamins under the skin) and core. Juice in the juicer.


# 9.48 Plum Cake

Cancer preventive effect, dehydrates the body, stimulates digestion and
binds fats in the intestine, good to fight loss of appetite, flatulence,
inflammatory bowel disease, obesity, gout, stomach ulcers, stomach
cramps, rheumatism, heartburn. Relieves pain, detoxifying, bactericide.
Cooking time approx. 1 hour
Allergens: AG
6 portions to 307,83g. / 502kcal. - (carb:71% / prot:29%)
100g.=163,24kcal. / protein 12,32g. fat:19,28g.
µg. - Ph:2,65 Na:0,77 Ka:5,44 Mg:0,5 Ca:0,87 Fe:0,03 Zn:0,02 Col.:0,05 Hsr.:1,38

**Quantity of ingredients:**
Curd cheese 20% 5/8 oz / 200g. (yes)
Wheat flour 7/8 lbs / 400g. (yes)
Cow's milk (whole milk 3.5% fat) 6 table spoons / 70g. (yes)
Rapeseed oil 6 table spoons / 70g. (yes)
Honey 8 table spoons / 100g. (little)
Baking powder 1 package / 3g. (yes)
Salt 1 pinch / 1g. (little)
Cinnamon ground 1 teaspoon / 3g. (yes)
Plums 2,2 lbs / 1000g. (yes)

**Cooking instructions:**
Mix the flour, curd cheese, milk, oil, honey, salt and baking powder into a smooth dough. Keep the dough cool for 15 minutes to cool.
Lay out baking paper on a baking sheet and press the dough out to a bottom. Now spread the plums evenly.
Sprinkle the cake with the cinnamon and bake for about 40 minutes at 190 ° C/374 °F.

# 9.49 Polenta with peach

Relieves fatigue, forcing spleen, diuretic, strengthens the defense, good to fight fungi infections, lets urine and bile juice flow, prevents the aging process, strengthens brain cells.
Cooking time approx. 20 min
3 portions to 254g. / 197kcal. - (carb:89% / prot:11%)
100g.=77,56kcal. / protein 4,48g. fat:0,6g.
µg. - Ph:2,76 Na:0,12 Ka:11,83 Mg:0,93 Ca:1,02 Fe:0,05 Zn:0,02 Col.:0 Hsr.:1,56

**Quantity of ingredients:**
Water 1 1/2 cups / 240g. (yes)
Corn Grease (Polenta) 1 cup / 120g. (yes)
Peaches 2-3 pieces / 400g. (yes)
Vanilla pod 1 pinch / 1g. (yes)
Chili (pod or ground) 1 pinch / 0,1g. (yes)
Cinnamon ground 1 pinch / 1g. (yes)

**Cooking instructions:**
Pour the polenta into a pan of hot water with constant stirring until the polenta has the desired consistency. Pull the polenta from the fire and let it soak for 10 minutes.
Wash fresh peaches and cut into quarters. Pour into the finished polenta the peaches, add the vanilla and add Chili to taste, stir and let it go for 3 minutes. Winter varieties: Pickled fruit, pear, apples.

## 9.50 Potato cream with herbs and fresh cheese

Good to fight loss of appetite, constipation, bloating and nausea.
Improves digestion, supports urination, prevents cancer, forcing spleen,
dissolves stagnation, relaxing and reassuring.
Cooking time approx. 25 min
Allergens: G
2 portions to 218,5g. / 217kcal. - (carb:14% / prot:86%)
100g.=99,31kcal. / protein 8,76g. fat:11,22g.
µg. - Ph:18,66 Na:18,04 Ka:73,64 Mg:4,87 Ca:13,9 Fe:0,13 Zn:0,09 Col.:4,84 Hsr.:2,24

**Quantity of ingredients:**
Potato (mealy) 5/8 lbs - 8oz / 250g. (yes)
Fresh cheese 3 oz / 80g. (yes)
Yogurt (natural, 1.5% fat) 3 table spoons / 45g. (yes)
Chives 1/2 bunch / 50g. (yes)
Basil (fresh) 1 teaspoon / 4g. (yes)
Parsley 1 teaspoon / 4g. (yes)
Dill 1/2 teaspoon / 2g. (yes)
Salt 1 pinch / 1g. (little)
Black caraway 1 pinch / 0,5g. (yes)
Pepper (ground) 1 pinch / 0,5g. ()

**Cooking instructions:**
Softly steam the potatoes in the pan, peel them and press through the
potato press.
Mix cream cheese, yoghurt and herbs under the potatoes, season with
salt, crushed black cumin and pepper.

## 9.51 Potato gnocchi with vegetables and basil sauce

Strengthens immune system, promotes weight loss. Good to fight
immunodeficiency, loss of appetite, flatulence, high blood pressure.
Relaxing and reassuring.
Cooking time approx. 1 hour
Allergens: ACGL
4 portions to 290,25g. / 167kcal. - (carb:75% / prot:25%)
100g.=57,45kcal. / protein 6,54g. fat:4,63g.
µg. - Ph:3,26 Na:1,11 Ka:13,57 Mg:2,45 Ca:9,39 Fe:0,06 Zn:0,02 Col.:1,36 Hsr.:1,49

**Quantity of ingredients:**
Potato 5/8 lbs - 8oz / 250g. (yes)
Wheat flour 1 oz / 25g. (yes)
Wheat semolina 1/2 oz / 15g. (yes)

Chicken yolk 1 piece / 20g. (yes)
Nutmeg 1 pinch / 0,2g. (yes)
Basic recipe for a vegetable soup (nutritious) 1 cup / 250g. (yes)
Celery root 1/8 lbs - 2oz / 50g. (yes)
Lemon peel 1/2 teaspoon / 2g. (yes)
Ginger fresh 1/2 teaspoon / 2g. (yes)
Nutmeg 1 pinch / 0,2g. (yes)
Basil (fresh) 1 Bunch / 125g. (yes)
Crème fraiche cheese 1 table spoon / 20g. (little)
Salt 1 pinch / 1g. (little)
Pepper (ground) 1 pinch / 0,2g. ()
Carrot 1/4 lbs - 4oz / 100g. (yes)
Zucchini 1/4 lbs - 4oz / 100g. (yes)
Cauliflower 1/4 lbs - 4oz / 100g. (yes)
Broccoli 1/4 lbs - 4oz / 100g. (yes)
Salt 1 pinch / 1g. (little)


**Cooking instructions:**
Steam the potatoes gently, peel and pass hot through the potato press.
Process the hot potatoes with flour, semolina, egg, nutmeg and salt to a
smooth dough. Let dough rest for 3o minutes.
Make small rolls (2 cm) out of the dough with flour-dusted hands, cut off
1 cm thin slices. To create the typical gnocchi shape, gently dab the
dough pieces with your thumb. Leave the gnocchi in lightly boiling
salted water for 6 - 8 minutes. Lift the gnocchi out of the pot with the
skimmer.

Heat the vegetable stock till it boils. Add diced celery, grated lemon
peel, finely chopped ginger and 1 pinch of nutmeg. Cover and simmer
for about 10 minutes. Using the blender, puree the vegetable broth,
celery, chopped basil and créme fraiche into a smooth sauce. Season
with salt and nutmeg.

Cut carrots, zucchini, cauliflower and broccoli into small pieces and
cook covered in a sieve over steam for 8 minutes until firm.
Heat the sauce again and add to the vegetables and arrange over the
gnocchi.

## 9.52 Potato pancakes

Promotes spleen, reduces inflammation, improves digestion, regenerates skin, supports urination, calms nerves and stomach, laxative, antiparasitic.
Cooking time approx. 15 min
Allergens: ACG
1 portion to 377g. / 893kcal. - (carb:17% / prot:83%)
100g.=236,87kcal. / protein 12,4g. fat:32,76g.
µg. - Ph:69,92 Na:22,7 Ka:275,07 Mg:17,98 Ca:27,85 Fe:0,58 Zn:0,44 Col.:45,38 Hsr.:15,19

**Quantity of ingredients:**
Potato (mealy) 5/8 lbs - 8oz / 250g. (yes)
Wheat flour 1/2 oz / 10g. (yes)
Chicken egg 1 piece / 35g. (yes)
Rapeseed oil 2 table spoons / 20g. (yes)
Salt 1 pinch / 1g. (little)
Cream sour 20% 1/8 lbs - 2oz / 50g. (little)
Salt 1 pinch / 1g. (little)
Herbs various 1 table spoon / 10g. (yes)

**Cooking instructions:**
Grater the peeled potatoes finely, add the remaining ingredients, mix well and salt. Heat the oil and add small flat cakes to the pan with the spoon. Roast the potato pancakes on both sides crispy golden brown. Place them on the
plate with sour cream, salt and sprinkle with herbs.

## 9.53 Potato-basil soup

Reduces inflammation, improves digestion, supports urination, lowers cholesterol, reduces blood pressure, strengthens immune system, prevents cancer, reduces radiation damage, antioxidative, dissolves stagnation.
Cooking time approx. 25 min
Allergens: L
4 portions to 330g. / 96kcal. - (carb:69% / prot:31%)
100g.=28,94kcal. / protein 3,23g. fat:2,99g.
µg. - Ph:1,91 Na:3,35 Ka:13,03 Mg:0,61 Ca:2,91 Fe:0,03 Zn:0,01 Col.:0 Hsr.:1,9

**Quantity of ingredients:**
Water 2 cups / 450g. (yes)
Potato 4 pieces / 200g. (yes)
Carrot 2 pieces / 100g. (yes)
Celery root 1 piece / 500g. (yes)
Pepper (ground) 1 pinch / 0,5g. ()
Ground 1 pinch / 1g. (yes)
Garlic 1 clove / 3g. (yes)
Salt 1 pinch / 1g. (little)
Lemon 1 teaspoon / 3g. (yes)
Basil (fresh) 1 Bunch / 50g. (yes)
Peppers powder 1 pinch / 1g. (yes)
Sugar cane sugar 1 pinch / 1g. (little)
Olive oil 1 table spoon / 10g. (yes)

**Cooking instructions:**
Peeled and chopped 4 medium potatoes in a pot of hot water and 2 chopped medium carrots, a piece of celery root, a pinch of pepper, a pinch of ground cumin, crushed a small clove of garlic, a pinch of salt, 1 teaspoon of lemon juice, simmer until the Vegetables is soft.

Add 1 bunch finely chopped basil into one half of the soup and puree everything; stir in the other half of the basil; with rose paprika, a pinch of whole cane sugar, 1 tablespoon of olive oil or butter, freshly ground pepper, salt to taste.

# 9.54 Pumpkin curry

Promotes digestion and sweating, Dissolves stagnation, strengthens lungs and spleen, diuretic, reduces blood glucose, forcing spleen and digestive system, detoxifying, strengthens the muscles and bones.
Cooking time approx. 20 min
3 portions to 251g. / 193kcal. - (carb:63% / prot:37%)
100g.=77,03kcal. / protein 2,72g. fat:10,61g.
µg. - Ph:5,14 Na:0,86 Ka:16,34 Mg:2,68 Ca:2,29 Fe:0,06 Zn:0,02 Col.:0 Hsr.:1,54

**Quantity of ingredients:**
Pumpkin 3/4 lbs / 300g. (yes)
Olive oil 2 table spoons / 30g. (yes)
Coriander 1 pinch / 1g. (yes)
Pepper (ground) 1 pinch / 0,5g. ()
Curry 1 pinch / 1g. (yes)
Water 1/4 cup / 50g. (yes)
Salt 1 pinch / 1g. (little)

Parsley 1 table spoon / 7g. (yes)
Cardamom 1 pinch / 1g. (yes)
Turmeric (yellow root) 1 pinch / 1g. (yes)
Rice (whole grain) 1/2 cup / 60g. (yes)
Water 3 cups / 300g. (yes)
Salt 1 pinch / 1g. (little)

**Cooking instructions:**
Heat olive oil in pan. Steam the pumpkin cut in cubes, season with cilantro, pepper and curry, simmer with a little water, salt with sea salt, add chopped parsley with cardamom and turmeric, simmer on a small fire for about 10 minutes, depending on the pumpkin, the pumpkin should still be firm.
Place the rice in salted water, bring to the boil and let it simmer over low heat for about 15 minutes.

## 9.55  Pumpkin slices with spicy rice

Strengthens lungs and spleen, diuretic, reduces blood glucose, protects liver, for the drainage of the body overweight and high blood pressure, harmonizes liver.
Cooking time approx. 45 min
Allergens: AG
4 portions to 260,5g. / 438kcal. - (carb:59% / prot:41%)
100g.=168,04kcal. / protein 4,2g. fat:27,77g.
µg. - Ph:4,8 Na:1,27 Ka:11,64 Mg:2,02 Ca:3,02 Fe:0,04 Zn:0,02 Col.:0,25 Hsr.:1,33

**Quantity of ingredients:**
Clarified butter 1/2 teaspoon / 5g. (little)
Saffron 1 Sachet / 0,1g. (yes)
Turmeric (yellow root) 1 teaspoon / 2g. (yes)
Rice Basmati 1 cup / 120g. (yes)
Water 1 cup / 120g. (yes)
Salt 1/2 teaspoon / 2g. (little)
Pumpkin 6-8 slices / 400g. (yes)
Barley flour 1 cup / 10g. (yes)
Breadcrumbs (wheat bread, bread roll) 1 cup / 10g. (yes)
Salt 1/2 teaspoon / 2g. (little)
Pepper (ground) 1 pinch / 1g. ()
Butter organic 1 table spoon / 10g. (little)
Cream, sweet 30% 1 1/2 cup / 300g. (little)
Barley flour 2 table spoons / 20g. (yes)
Chives 3 table spoons / 20g. (yes)
Dill 3 table spoons / 20g. (yes)

**Cooking instructions:**
Melt the fat in a small saucepan, add saffron and turmeric, lightly roast over medium heat for about 1-2 minutes to allow the aromas to develop (note: the spices should never be burnt). Add the rice for about 2 minutes stir fry, add the salt, stir briefly and add the water, stir and close the pot with a lid. Cook at low to medium heat until the water is almost completely absorbed, then remove from the heat and set aside with the lid still closed and let it swell. Do not stir! When the water is completely absorbed, the rice is ready!

Mix flour, bread crumbs, salt and pepper. Moisten the pumpkin slices with water or mashed egg, turn the slices in the flour mixture and fry gently in butter until golden brown and the pumpkin is soft. Melt the butter in a small saucepan, brown the barley flour in it and remove from heat, add the sour cream, season with salt, pepper, add the chopped herbs and pour the sauce over the fried pumpkin slices. Serve with the rice.

## 9.56 Pumpkin soup

Promotes digestion, forcing spleen and stomach, reduces blood pressure, strengthens immune system, prevents cancer, reduces radiation damage, improves digestion, regenerates skin, lowers cholesterol, reduces blood glucose, protects liver.
Cooking time approx. 1 hour
3 portions to 236,33g. / 105kcal. - (carb:71% / prot:29%)
100g.=44,29kcal. / protein 2,54g. fat:3,64g.
µg. - Ph:4,02 Na:0,96 Ka:24,72 Mg:1,82 Ca:2,89 Fe:0,08 Zn:0,02 Col.:0 Hsr.:1,08

**Quantity of ingredients:**
Pumpkin 3/4 lbs / 300g. (yes)
Carrot 2 pieces / 100g. (yes)
Potato 2 pieces / 120g. (yes)
Olive oil 1 table spoon / 10g. (yes)
Onion white 1 piece / 50g. (yes)
Water 1 cup / 120g. (yes)
Parsley 1 table spoon / 7g. (yes)
Anise (Common Fennel) 1 pinch / 1g. (yes)
Salt 1 pinch / 1g. (little)

**Cooking instructions:**
Add the olive oil to the pan, add the diced pumpkin, diced carrots and potatoes. Roast them shortly, add the finely chopped onion, fill with water, add enough water to cover the vegetables at least 3 finger-widths. Boil at low heat.
Season with sea salt, add small cutted parsley, a pinch of anise (little). Allow to simmer for about 35 minutes. Then purée the soup and add some water, depending on the consistency of the soup.

## 9.57 Pumpkin-yoghurt soup

Relaxes, reduces blood pressure, strengthens immune system, promotes weight loss. Good to fight immunodeficiency, loss of appetite, flatulence, depressions, diabetes, diarrhea.
Cooking time approx. 15 min
Allergens: GL
4 portions to 239g. / 68kcal. - (carb:83% / prot:17%)
100g.=28,45kcal. / protein 2,37g. fat:1,31g.
µg. - Ph:1,79 Na:0,9 Ka:6,6 Mg:2,8 Ca:10,96 Fe:0,02 Zn:0,01 Col.:0,05 Hsr.:0,35

**Quantity of ingredients:**
Basic recipe for a vegetable soup (nutritious) 1 cup / 300g. (yes)
Hokkaido pumpkin 1,1 lbs / 500g. (yes)
Ginger fresh 1/2 teaspoon / 2g. (yes)
Fennel seeds ground 1/2 teaspoon / 1g. (yes)
Anise (Common Fennel) 1/4 teaspoon / 1g. (yes)
Yogurt (natural, 1.5% fat) 3/8 lbs - 6oz / 150g. (yes)
Peppermint 2 leaves / 1g. (yes)
Salt 1 pinch / 1g. (little)

**Cooking instructions:**
Heat the vegetable broth (after the basic recipe) till it boils. Add diced pumpkin, chopped ginger, crushed fennel seeds and anise. Bring the soup to the boil and simmer for about 12 minutes until the pumpkin is soft.
Remove soup from the heat. Puree the soup with the yoghurt with the blender. Serve soup with finely chopped mint sprinkled.

## 9.58 Quick zucchini soup

Diuretic, supports urination. Strengthens gastrointestinal function, expands blood vessels, prevents cancer, prevents diseases (in the elderly). Stimulates liver function, detoxifying.
Cooking time approx. 10 min
4 portions to 241,5g. / 42kcal. - (carb:46% / prot:54%)
100g.=17,29kcal. / protein 1,76g. fat:2,04g.
µg. - Ph:3,81 Na:0,41 Ka:29,78 Mg:3,2 Ca:5,37 Fe:0,21 Zn:0,01 Col.:0 Hsr.:2,85

**Quantity of ingredients:**
Zucchini 2-3 pieces / 500g. (yes)
Onion white 1 piece / 50g. (yes)
Corn germ oil 2 table spoons / 6g. (yes)
Parsley 1 table spoon / 7g. (yes)
Chives 1 teaspoon / 3g. (yes)
Water 2 cup / 400g. (yes)

**Cooking instructions:**
Fry chopped onion in oil. Add sliced zucchini and sauté well. Pour with water. Chop parsley and chives, add and puree everything.

## 9.59 Radish, apple and yogurt fresh food

Stops diarrhea, promotes digestion, appetizing, detoxifying, supports urination, reduces thirst, prevents cancer, strengthens body cells, dissolves stagnation.
Cooking time approx. 10 min
Allergens: G
2 portions to 160g. / 77kcal. - (carb:79% / prot:21%)
100g.=48,12kcal. / protein 2,03g. fat:1,39g.
µg. - Ph:9,35 Na:4,33 Ka:62,52 Mg:3,01 Ca:12,05 Fe:0,2 Zn:0,06 Col.:0,55 Hsr.:3,13

**Quantity of ingredients:**
Yogurt (natural, 3.5% fat) 5 table spoons / 50g. (yes)
Lemon juice 1/2 teaspoon / 2g. (yes)
Salt 1 pinch / 0,5g. (little)
Pepper white (ground) 1 pinch / 0,1g. (yes)
Radish (white, green, purple-red) 1/4 lbs - 4oz / 100g. (yes)
Apple (sweet) 1 piece / 150g. (yes)
Parsley 2 table spoons / 18g. (yes)

**Cooking instructions:**
Mix yoghurt with lemon juice, salt and white pepper.

Wash radish and apple, peel and finely grate. Mix with the yoghurt sauce, let it pass briefly. Sprinkle with chopped parsley.


## 9.60 Refreshing cucumber soup with potatoes

Diuretic, detoxifying, suppresses conversion of sugar into fat, lowers cholesterol, prevents cancer, reduces inflammation, improves digestion, lowers cholesterol, dissolves stagnation, improves blood circulation, stimulates appetite.
Cooking time approx. 15 min
Allergens: GN
3 portions to 307,33g. / 148kcal. - (carb:70% / prot:30%)
100g.=48,26kcal. / protein 3,93g. fat:5,09g.
µg. - Ph:3,72 Na:0,77 Ka:23,54 Mg:1,43 Ca:2 Fe:0,05 Zn:0,02 Col.:0 Hsr.:1,19

**Quantity of ingredients:**
Sesame oil 1 table spoon / 10g. (yes)
Potato 4 pieces / 300g. (yes)
Onion (spring onion) 3 pieces / 60g. (yes)
Pepper (ground) 1 pinch / 0,5g. ()
Nutmeg 1 pinch / 1g. (yes)
Salt 1 pinch / 1g. (little)
Lemon 1/2 piece / 25g. (yes)
Cucumber 2 pieces / 500g. (yes)
Cream, sweet 30% 1 table spoon / 10g. (little)
Dill 1 table spoon / 15g. (yes)

**Cooking instructions:**
Sauté sesame oil, chopped potatoes, plenty of spring onions in a hot pot; add pepper, a little nutmeg, salt, lemon juice, hot water, diced cucumber; simmer for about 10 minutes and then puree; add some sweet cream as you like,
and fresh dill.

Variation: Add a little chili, oregano, thyme or rosemary to soften the cooling effect.

## 9.61 Rhubarb and apple jelly

Antioxidants, lots of vitamin C, laxative, relieves pain, detoxifying, warms stomach and spleen, improves blood circulation.
Cooking time approx. 15 min
2 portions to 276,5g. / 180kcal. - (carb:96% / prot:4%)
100g.=65,1kcal. / protein 1,19g. fat:0,58g.
µg. - Ph:14,75 Na:1,5 Ka:93,5 Mg:7,42 Ca:12,73 Fe:0,29 Zn:0,07 Col.:0 Hsr.:6,21

### Quantity of ingredients:
Rhubarb 5/8 oz / 200g. (yes)
Apple juice (natural cloudy) 1 cup / 300g. (little)
Corn starch 1 oz / 30g. (yes)
Honey 1/2 oz / 20g. (little)
Vanilla sugar natural 1 pinch / 0,5g. (little)
Cinnamon ground 1 pinch / 0,5g. (yes)
Peppermint 2 leaves / 2g. (yes)

### Cooking instructions:
Add the cornstarch to a 1/2 cup apple juice.
Simmer the rhubarb in 1 cup of water for 10 min.
Add the remaining apple juice and the cornstarch, stir, heat till it boils again.
Sweet with honey and season with vanilla and cinnamon. Spread the mixture on dessert bowls and garnish with mint.

## 9.62 Rice congee with carrots and fennel

Worms, forcing spleen, relieves constipation, stimulates nerves, detoxifying, reduces inflammation, improves blood circulation, reduces blood pressure, strengthens immune system, prevents cancer, reduces radiation damage.
Cooking time approx. 2 hours and more
Allergens: G
3 portions to 284,67g. / 131kcal. - (carb:94% / prot:6%)
100g.=46,14kcal. / protein 4,17g. fat:1,37g.
µg. - Ph:3,26 Na:3,23 Ka:18,37 Mg:21,62 Ca:22,98 Fe:0,13 Zn:0,03 Col.:0,09 Hsr.:1,26

### Quantity of ingredients:
Basic recipe for a rice soup (Congee) 2 cup / 500g. (yes)
Carrot 2 pieces / 100g. (yes)
Fennel 1 piece / 250g. (yes)
Butter organic 1 teaspoon / 3g. (little)
Cardamom 1/2 teaspoon / 1g. (yes)

**Cooking instructions:**
Cook rice congee according to basic recipe.
Clean and cut carrots and fennel.

When carrots and fennel are cooked from the beginning, they serve wholesomeness. If added shortly before the end of the cooking time, taste and vitamins are retained.

Refine with butter and cardamom before serving.

## 9.63 Rice congee with honey pear and black sesame

Promotes digestion, supports urination, good to fight blood circulation disorders, thromboses, risk of embolism, high blood pressure, a headache, heart attack and stroke.
Cooking time approx. 10 min - 3 hours
Allergens: N
2 portions to 271,5g. / 158kcal. - (carb:95% / prot:5%)
100g.=58,38kcal. / protein 2,43g. fat:1,55g.
µg. - Ph:4,8 Na:0,43 Ka:18,44 Mg:35,15 Ca:34,31 Fe:0,09 Zn:0,06 Col.:0 Hsr.:2,88

**Quantity of ingredients:**
Basic recipe for a rice soup (Congee) 1 1/2 cups / 240g. (yes)
Pear 2 pieces / 300g. (yes)
Sesame, black 1 teaspoon / 3g. (yes)

**Cooking instructions:**
Cook rice congee according to basic recipe.
Fill pot with 3 cm of water and heat till it boils. Quarter the pears (with the skin and seeds) and simmer them covered with black sesame for 10 minutes. Mix with the rice.

## 9.64 Roasted barley patties

Improves digestion, lowers cholesterol, good to fight diarrhea, ulceration, joint pain, stomach problems. Promotes spleen and liver, reduces blood pressure, strengthens immune system, prevents cancer, reduces radiation damage, stimulates liver function.
Cooking time approx. 1 1/2 hours
Allergens: ACN
3 portions to 292,67g. / 398kcal. - (carb:63% / prot:37%)
100g.=135,99kcal. / protein 8,38g. fat:19,69g.
µg. - Ph:7,07 Na:4,18 Ka:17,24 Mg:2,02 Ca:2,5 Fe:0,08 Zn:0,04 Col.:2,76 Hsr.:2,93

**Quantity of ingredients:**
Water 1 1/2 cups / 250g. (yes)
Barley grouts 1 cup / 120g. (yes)
Potato 1 piece / 140g. (yes)
Carrot 1 piece / 120g. (yes)
Champignon 2-3 pieces / 25g. (yes)
Chicken egg 1 piece / 55g. (yes)
Onion white 1 piece / 50g. (yes)
Ginger fresh 1/2 teaspoon / 1g. (yes)
Pepper (ground) 1 pinch / 0,5g. ()
Salt 1 pinch / 1g. (little)
Lemon 1/2 piece / 15g. (yes)
Parsley 2 table spoons / 15g. (yes)
Peppers powder 1 pinch / 1g. (yes)
Sesame oil 2 table spoons / 50g. (yes)
Bread roll 1 piece / 35g. (little)

**Cooking instructions:**
Preparation:
Place 2 large cups of hot water in a saucepan; add 1 large cup of barley porridge; simmer for 2 minutes while stirring; then let it swell for 20 minutes on the switched off stove; take down and let cool.
Cook in boiling water 1 large potato, chopped and cut.
Soak 1 roll in hot water and squeeze well.
Then: Mix the barley groats and crushed the potato. Add 1 grated carrot, 2 - 3 chopped mushrooms, 1 egg, 1 finely chopped onion, 1/2 teaspoon grated ginger, a pinch of pepper, a pinch of salt, a little lemon juice, chopped parsley, plenty of rose paprika; knead well and form patties; heat sesame oil in a hot pan; fry the patties for about 15 minutes over a gentle heat; turn at half time.
Also fits well: lettuce, soybean vegetables.

## 9.65 Roasted millet with plum compote

Supports urination, promotes spleen and kidney, strengthens the defense. Good to fight fungi infections.
Cooking time approx. 30 min
4 portions to 218,25g. / 139kcal. - (carb:85% / prot:15%)
100g.=63,8kcal. / protein 3,57g. fat:1,24g.
µg. - Ph:2,99 Na:0,1 Ka:4,37 Mg:1,68 Ca:0,78 Fe:0,09 Zn:0,03 Col.:0 Hsr.:0,93

**Quantity of ingredients:**
Millet 1 cup / 120g. (yes)
Water 1 1/2 cups / 250g. (yes)
Plum 1 1/2 cups / 250g. (yes)
Vanilla pod 1 pinch / 1g. (yes)
Water 5/8 lbs - 8oz / 250g. (yes)
Cinnamon ground 1 pinch / 1g. (yes)
Acerola fruit nectar or powder 1/2 teaspoon / 1g. (little)

**Cooking instructions:**
Roast millet briefly, pour over water, heat till it boils and let stand for 20 min. to swell.

Cook plums with water, vanilla and cinnamon 10 min. then strain. Add acerola and add to the millet.

# 9.66 Rosemary Potatoes

Reduces Inflammation, improves digestion, regenerates skin, supports urination, lowers cholesterol. Rosemary stimulates digestion, strengthens lung, promotes spleen and kidney, dries out.
Cooking time approx. 30 min
2 portions to 216,5g. / 188kcal. - (carb:76% / prot:24%)
100g.=87,07kcal. / protein 4,21g. fat:5,25g.
µg. - Ph:11,51 Na:0,72 Ka:82,88 Mg:4,72 Ca:1,86 Fe:0,1 Zn:0,07 Col.:0 Hsr.:3,64

**Quantity of ingredients:**
Potato 6-8 pieces / 420g. (yes)
Salt (herbal) 1 pinch / 1g. (little)
Olive oil 1 table spoon / 10g. (yes)
Rosemary 1 teaspoon / 2g. (yes)

**Cooking instructions:**
Cut the potatoes into half´s, apply a little olive oil on the cut surface, then salt, sprinkle 2 - 3 rosemary needles on the potatoes.
Place the potatoes on the baking tray and bake them in the preheated oven for approx. 25 minutes to 190°C/374°F.

## 9.67 Scrambled eggs with leaf salad olives and tomatoes

Calms nerves and stomach, relieves fatigue, regulates gastrointestinal function, promotes digestion, stimulates liver function, detoxifying, helps to digest fat, supports urination, reduces blood pressure.
Cooking time approx. 10 min
Allergens: C
1 portion to 264g. / 419kcal. - (carb:8% / prot:92%)
100g.=158,71kcal. / protein 24,4g. fat:33,87g.
µg. - Ph:158,54 Na:226,49 Ka:184,78 Mg:13,81 Ca:53,55 Fe:1,72 Zn:1,03 Col.:270,04
Hsr.:7,46

**Quantity of ingredients:**
Chicken egg 2-3 pieces / 180g. (yes)
Olive oil 1 table spoon / 10g. (yes)
Salt 1 pinch / 1g. (little)
Pepper (ground) 1 pinch / 0,5g. ()
Olives 6 pieces / 10g. (yes)
Tomato 1 piece / 50g. (yes)
Lettuce 2 leaves / 5g. (rec.)
Turmeric (yellow root) 1 pinch / 1g. (yes)
Parsley 1/2 teaspoon / 5g. (yes)
Basil (fresh) 2-3 leaves / 2g. (yes)

**Cooking instructions:**
Heat olive oil in the pan. Cut the tomato into a slice. Pluck salad into small pieces. Briefly fry tomatoes, lettuce and olives. Meanwhile mix eggs with salt and spices with a fork.
Pour the egg and spices into the pan. Stir with a wooden spoon until it reaches the desired consistency.
Spices and herbs: turmeric, parsley, basil, black cumin
Variation: zucchini, rocket

## 9.68 Scrambled eggs with rocket and herbs

Calms nerves and stomach, promotes digestion, detoxifying, promotes perspiration, reduces blood lipids, stimulates, stimulates liver function, harmonizes liver and spleen, strengthens eyesight, detoxifying.
Cooking time approx. 10 min
Allergens: CG
1 portion to 191g. / 360kcal. - (carb:11% / prot:89%)
100g.=188,48kcal. / protein 16,61g. fat:30,38g.
µg. - Ph:156,1 Na:98,06 Ka:229,29 Mg:15,37 Ca:66,01 Fe:1,96 Zn:0,98 Col.:273,93
Hsr.:9,63

**Quantity of ingredients:**
Butter organic 2 table spoons / 20g. (little)
Ginger fresh 1 knife tip / 1g. (yes)
Chicken egg 2 pieces / 120g. (yes)
Pepper (ground) 1 pinch / 0,5g. ()
Coriander 1 pinch / 1g. (yes)
Parsley 2 table spoons / 16g. (yes)
Oregano dried 1 teaspoon / 2g. (yes)
Savory 1 pinch / 0,5g. (yes)

**Cooking instructions:**
Melt a piece of butter in a hot pan; add fine cutted ginger and roast it shortly. Mix in 1 egg whipped, pepper freshly ground, a pinch of coriander, bean cabbage, some salt, parsley chopped, rocket and oregano cut into small pieces until the egg stalls, but still juicy. Garnish: millet, polenta, potatoes, toasted bread. The dish is wholesome, without carbohydrate.

## 9.69 Semolina soup with vegetables

Reduces blood pressure, strengthens immune system, prevents cancer, forcing spleen, dissolves stagnation, promotes weight loss. Good to fight immunodeficiency, loss of appetite, flatulence, high blood pressure, depressions, diabetes, diarrhea, rheumatism, heartburn, twelffinger intestinal ulcers.
Cooking time approx. 20 min
Allergens: AGL
3 portions to 237,67g. / 105kcal. - (carb:85% / prot:15%)
100g.=44,32kcal. / protein 2,38g. fat:4,24g.
µg. - Ph:2,88 Na:3,04 Ka:8,54 Mg:9,5 Ca:37,49 Fe:0,11 Zn:0,03 Col.:0 Hsr.:1,7

**Quantity of ingredients:**
Basic recipe for a vegetable soup (nutritious) 2 cup / 500g. (yes)
Wheat semolina 2 table spoons / 20g. (yes)
Lovage 1/2 teaspoon / 2g. (yes)
Basil (fresh) 1/2 teaspoon / 1g. (yes)
Nutmeg 1 pinch / 0,1g. (yes)
Carrot 1/4 lbs - 4oz / 100g. (yes)
Celery root 1/8 lbs - 2oz / 50g. (yes)
Cream, sweet 30% 3 table spoons / 30g. (little)
Parsley 1 table spoon / 10g. (yes)

**Cooking instructions:**
Roast wheat grits without fat in a pan. Roast the chopped carrots and celery briefly. Add the vegetable soup (Basic recipe for a vegetable soup). Season with lovage, nutmeg and let it 10 min. simmer. Stir in the cream before serving and garnish with parsley.

## 9.70 Spelled with fruit and nuts

Stops diarrhea, promotes digestion, appetizing, relieves fatigue, anti-inflammatory (gastrointestinal). Good to fight tumor lesions and leukemia, is antiallergic in food allergies, regulates metabolism, lowers blood glucose and cholesterol.
Cooking time approx. 1 1/2 hours
Allergens: AH
3 portions to 286,33g. / 290kcal. - (carb:76% / prot:24%)
100g.=101,16kcal. / protein 8,64g. fat:6,67g.
µg. - Ph:9,7 Na:8,81 Ka:25,53 Mg:3,53 Ca:2,83 Fe:0,14 Zn:0,02 Col.:0 Hsr.:2,96

**Quantity of ingredients:**
Spelled grain 1 cup / 120g. (yes)
Water 1 cup / 50g. (yes)
Apple (sweet) 1 piece / 220g. (yes)
Apricot 1 piece / 200g. (yes)
Peaches 1 piece / 120g. (yes)
Cinnamon ground 1 pinch / 1g. (yes)
Cardamom 1 pinch / 1g. (yes)
Salt 1 pinch / 1g. (little)
Strawberries 1 cup / 120g. (yes)
Almond puree 1 table spoon / 15g. (yes)
Cocoa 1 pinch / 1g. (yes)
Walnuts 1 table spoon / 10g. (yes)

**Cooking instructions:**
Put spelled in hot water and cook.

Then: Give sweet chopped fruit (apples, apricots, peaches) in a little hot water, with a little cinnamon, sauté briefly; ground cardamom and / or coriander, a small pinch of salt, the boiled spelled, berries after season. Put some cocoa and roasted nuts over it.

## 9.71 Spicy avocado cream with cottage cheese

Anti-inflammatory, good to fight swelling, pain and itching, forcing spleen and digestive system, detoxifying, bactericide.
Cooking time approx. 15 min
Allergens: G
4 portions to 271,25g. / 614kcal. - (carb:39% / prot:61%)
100g.=226,27kcal. / protein 11,04g. fat:40,92g.
µg. - Ph:7,44 Na:14,84 Ka:19,28 Mg:1,27 Ca:2,23 Fe:0,03 Zn:0,03 Col.:0,06 Hsr.:1,09

**Quantity of ingredients:**
Avocado 2 pieces / 600g. (little)
Pepper (ground) 1 pinch / 0,5g. ()
Salt 1 pinch / 1g. (little)
Lemon juice 1/2 piece / 15g. (yes)
Peppers powder 1 pinch / 1g. (yes)
Olive oil 1 table spoon / 10g. (yes)
Chili (pod or ground) 1 pinch / 0,5g. (yes)
Herbs various 1 table spoon / 7g. (yes)
Cottage cheese 1 cup / 250g. (yes)
Bread with carob kernel flour 8 slices / 200g. (yes)

**Cooking instructions:**
Peel, core and purée avocados; add plenty of ground pepper, salt, lemon juice, rose paprika, a few drops of oil, chili, fresh chopped herbs, a pinch of salt; cottage cheese (about the same amount as avocado cream), carefully submerge.

Goes well with: Potatoes and millet, with which the avocado cream in combination with vegetable dishes, legumes or lettuce leaves a delicious meal. It is also very good as an appetizer, as a souvenir at parties and as a morning meal in the summer together with a mild dish of lentils or Adzuki beans and grated radish.

## 9.72 Spicy Tofu Vegetable Pan

Forcing spleen, relieves constipation, detoxifying, reduces inflammation, improves blood circulation, promotes sweating, dissolves stagnation, reduces flatulence, reduces blood pressure, strengthens immune system, prevents cancer, reduces radiation damage.
Cooking time approx. 25 min
Allergens: EN
4 portions to 329,25g. / 241kcal. - (carb:67% / prot:33%)
100g.=73,27kcal. / protein 7,37g. fat:7,32g.
µg. - Ph:3,76 Na:4,32 Ka:9,86 Mg:2,38 Ca:3,32 Fe:0,08 Zn:0,02 Col:0,01 Hsr.:1,82

**Quantity of ingredients:**
Sesame oil 2 table spoons / 20g. (yes)
Carrot 2 pieces / 100g. (yes)
Fennel 1 piece / 250g. (yes)
Leek 1 piece / 200g. (yes)
Salt 1 pinch / 1g. (little)
Turmeric (yellow root) 1 pinch / 1g. (yes)
Lemon juice 1 splash / 1g. (yes)
Soy Tofu 1 package / 120g. (yes)
Pepper (ground) 1 pinch / 0,5g. ()
Soy sauce 1 dash / 3g. (yes)
Rice (whole grain) 1 cup / 120g. (yes)
Water 6 cups / 500g. (yes)
Salt 1 pinch / 1g. (little)

**Cooking instructions:**
Heat sesame oil in a hot wok or a hot pan; fry the chopped carrots, fennel and leek slices; salt, a dash of lemon juice, turmeric, tofu cubes roast for 1 - 2 minutes.
Add the pepper and cook covered for about 5 minutes; drizzle with soy sauce.
Place the rice in salted water, heat till it boils and let it simmer over low heat for about 15 minutes.

# 9.73 Spring salad

Blood-forming, blood detoxifying, diuretic, good to fight stomach discomfort, improves digestion, diarrhea, helps to digest fat, supports urination, reduces blood pressure, detoxifying, reduces inflammation, diuretic.
Cooking time approx. 10 min
Allergens: AEMNO
4 portions to 214,25g. / 180kcal. - (carb:64% / prot:36%)
100g.=84,13kcal. / protein 7,68g. fat:5,56g.
µg. - Ph:14,38 Na:19,94 Ka:78,76 Mg:7,01 Ca:20,61 Fe:0,72 Zn:0,03 Col.:0 Hsr.:7,87

**Quantity of ingredients:**
Sorrel 3/8 lbs - 6oz / 150g. (yes)
Dandelion (young plants) 1/4 lbs - 4oz / 100g. (yes)
Mung bean sprouting 0,2 lbs / 75g. (yes)
Cress 1/4 lbs - 4oz / 100g. (yes)
Chives 1 Bunch / 50g. (yes)
Tomato 2 pieces / 100g. (yes)

Parsley 1 Bunch / 50g. (yes)
Sesame paste (Tahini) 2 table spoons / 16g. (yes)
Soy sauce 1 dash / 3g. (yes)
Mustard 1/2 teaspoon / 2g. (yes)
White bread (wheat bread) 6 slices / 120g. (little)
Vinegar Aceto Balsamico 1 table spoon / 8g. (yes)
Olive oil 1 table spoon / 8g. (yes)

**Cooking instructions:**
Wash all salad´s, mix and prepare the sauce as follows:
Mix tahini with mustard and balsamic vinegar, tamari, olive oil, chives
and half of parsley. Pour the sauce over the salad and sprinkle the
remaining parsley just before serving.
Serve with the white bread.

## 9.74 Tea from chamomile

Good to fight flatulence, nausea, intestinal cramps, diarrhea,
inflammation of the oral mucosa, influenza infections, stomach and
intestinal mucosa infections, badly healing wounds, nausea, colds, skin
rashes, inflammation in the genital and anal area.
Cooking time approx. 10 min
1 portion to 123g. / 0kcal. - (carb:0% / prot:0%)
100g.=0kcal. / protein 0g. fat:0g.
µg. - Ph:0 Na:0,98 Ka:0 Mg:0,98 Ca:4,88 Fe:0,01 Zn:0,1 Col.:0 Hsr.:0

**Quantity of ingredients:**
Chamomile 1 teaspoon / 3g. (yes)
Water 1 cup / 120g. (yes)

**Cooking instructions:**
Heat the water till it boils and put it aside. Chamomile flowers added
and 10 min. to let go.

## 9.75 Tea from elderberry blossom tea

Good, if you have a sore throat. Good to fight colds. Promotes urination,
good to fight flu, urinary stones, concentration weakness, blackheads,
hay fever, rheumatism. Strengthen the immune system, diaphoretic.
Cooking time approx. 10 min
4 portions to 128g. / 7kcal. - (carb:0% / prot:0%)
100g.=5,47kcal. / protein 0g. fat:0g.
µg. - Ph:0 Na:0,06 Ka:0 Mg:0,06 Ca:0,3 Fe:0 Zn:0,01 Col.:0 Hsr.:0

**Quantity of ingredients:**
Elderberry blossom tee 4 teaspoons / 12g. (yes)
Water 2 cup / 500g. (yes)

**Cooking instructions:**
Heat the water till it boils and put it aside. Add elderberry blossom tea and 10 min. to let go. Sweet to taste with honey. Strain when pouring.

## 9.76 Tea from ginger with honey

Honey relieves pain, detoxifying, bactericide.
Fresh ginger encourages digestion, detoxifying, strengthens bodily production, promotes perspiration, reduces blood lipids, stimulates, dissolves stagnation.
Cooking time approx. 30 min
4 portions to 127,25g. / 5kcal. - (carb:98% / prot:2%)
100g.=3,73kcal. / protein 0,01g. fat:0g.
µg. - Ph:0,02 Na:0,07 Ka:0,17 Mg:0,08 Ca:0,32 Fe:0 Zn:0,01 Col.:0 Hsr.:0

**Quantity of ingredients:**
Ginger fresh 1 teaspoon / 3g. (yes)
Water 2 cup / 500g. (yes)
Honey 2 teaspoons / 6g. (little)

**Cooking instructions:**
Heat the water till it boils and put it aside. Add ginger and 20-30 min. to let go. Sweet to taste with honey.

## 9.77 Tea mixture against general exhaustion

Good to fight general exhaustion. Antibacterial, encouragingly, good to fight loss of appetite, flatulence, heartburn.
Cooking time approx. 10 min
4 portions to 127g. / 2kcal. - (carb:55% / prot:45%)
100g.=1,57kcal. / protein 0,17g. fat:0,04g.
µg. - Ph:0,46 Na:0,43 Ka:3,71 Mg:0,53 Ca:2,53 Fe:0 Zn:0,03 Col.:0 Hsr.:0

**Quantity of ingredients:**
Lemon Balm (dried) 2 teaspoons / 3g. (yes)
Blackberry leaves 2 teaspoons / 3g. (yes)
Lavender blossoms 1 teaspoon / 2g. (yes)
Water 1 1/2 cups / 500g. (yes)

**Cooking instructions:**
Heat the water till it boils and put it aside. Add 2 g lemon balm, 2 g blackberry leaves, 1,5g lavender flowers, leave to stand covered for 10 minutes, then strain. Drink a cup three times a day.

## 9.78 Tea mixture appetizing

Ginger powder is warming, promotes sweating, dissolves stagnation.
Cooking time approx. 10 min
4 portions to 127,5g. / 0kcal. - (carb:83% / prot:17%)
100g.=0,39kcal. / protein 0,01g. fat:0g.
µg. - Ph:0,02 Na:0,06 Ka:0,12 Mg:0,08 Ca:0,32 Fe:0 Zn:0,01 Col.:0 Hsr.:0

**Quantity of ingredients:**
Bitter orange peel 1 teaspoons / 3g. (yes)
Yarrow tea 1 teaspoons / 3g. (yes)
Ginger powder 1g. Or 0,034oz / 1g. (yes)
Horehound leaves 1 teaspoons / 3g. (yes)
Water 2 cups / 500g. (yes)

**Cooking instructions:**
Brew one tablespoon of tea mixture with half a liter of water and leave for 10 min. to let go. Then strain and drink in small sips before eating.

## 9.79 Tomato soup

Promotes digestion, helps to digest fat, supports urination, reduces blood pressure, dissolves stagnation. Contains unsaturated fatty acids, is antioxidative.
Cooking time approx. 10 min
2 portions to 290g. / 100kcal. - (carb:42% / prot:58%)
100g.=34,66kcal. / protein 1,78g. fat:7,9g.
µg. - Ph:4,2 Na:1,2 Ka:31,36 Mg:1,99 Ca:3,85 Fe:0,07 Zn:0,04 Col.:0,01 Hsr.:1,47

**Quantity of ingredients:**
Olive oil 1 table spoon / 15g. (yes)
Onion white 1 piece / 60g. (yes)
Cinnamon ground 1 pinch / 1g. (yes)
Basil (fresh) 1 teaspoon / 2g. (yes)
Pepper (ground) 1 pinch / 0,5g. ()
Salt 1 pinch / 1g. (little)
Tomato 6 pieces / 250g. (yes)
Water 5/8 lbs - 8oz / 250g. (yes)
Peppers powder 1 pinch / 1g. (yes)

**Cooking instructions:**
Roast the onion in a pot. Salt and spices. Briefly roast. Put washed and quartered tomatoes in the pan. Stir and sauté briefly. Add a quart of water and heat till it boils. Cook for a quarter of an hour and puree.

## 9.80 Vanilla cream with berries

Weakness, chronic constipation of the intestine, weight loss, laxative, detoxifying, blood detoxifying. Strengthens the defense. Good to fight fungi infections.
Cooking time approx. 15 min
Allergens: G
4 portions to 272g. / 278kcal. - (carb:24% / prot:76%)
100g.=102,21kcal. / protein 13,82g. fat:31,13g.
µg. - Ph:5,99 Na:1,61 Ka:8,18 Mg:0,86 Ca:5,24 Fe:0,03 Zn:0,02 Col.:1,06 Hsr.:0,45

**Quantity of ingredients:**
Curd cheese 20% 7/8 lbs / 400g. (yes)
Yogurt (natural, 1.5% fat) 3/8 lbs - 6oz / 150g. (yes)
Sugar brown 2 teaspoons / 8g. (little)
Acerola fruit nectar or powder 1 teaspoon / 2g. (little)
Vanilla sugar natural 3 package / 3g. (little)
Cream (30% fat) 1/4 lbs - 4oz / 125g. (little)
Strawberries 1/4 lbs - 4oz / 100g. (yes)
Raspberry 1/4 lbs - 4oz / 100g. (yes)
Blackberry´s 1/4 lbs - 4oz / 100g. (yes)
Blueberry 1/4 lbs - 4oz / 100g. (yes)

**Cooking instructions:**
Mix the curd cheese, yoghurt, sugar, acerola and vanilla sugar with a hand mixer or whisk until smooth. Beat the whipped cream very stiff, mix it under the cream. Arrange vanilla cream in portions with the berries.

## 9.81 Vegetable bowl with Provencal pistou

Promotes spleen and liver, reduces blood pressure, strengthens immune system, prevents cancer, reduces radiation damage, forcing spleen, dissolves stagnation. Relieves constipation, strengthens mother milk production.
Cooking time approx. 1 1/2 hours
Allergens: AGL
8 portions to 323,12g. / 138kcal. - (carb:75% / prot:25%)
100g.=42,67kcal. / protein 5,89g. fat:6,34g.
µg. - Ph:0,65 Na:0,64 Ka:2,48 Mg:1,06 Ca:4,28 Fe:0,02 Zn:0 Col.:0,01 Hsr.:0,25

**Quantity of ingredients:**
Tomato 5/8 oz / 200g. (yes)
Olive oil 2 table spoons / 30g. (yes)
Garlic 1 clove / 5g. (yes)
Toast bread (whole grain) 1 slice / 5g. (yes)
Parmesan 1 oz / 30g. (little)
Basil (fresh) 1 Bunch / 125g. (yes)
Salt 1 pinch / 2g. (little)
Pepper (ground) 1 pinch / 1g. ()
Oregano dried 1 teaspoon / 3g. (yes)
Basic recipe for a vegetable soup (nutritious) 3 lbs / 1250g. (yes)
Carrot 3/8 lbs - 6oz / 150g. (yes)
Celery root 1/4 lbs - 4oz / 100g. (yes)
Broccoli 5/8 oz / 200g. (yes)
Fennel 1 piece / 250g. (yes)
Thyme dried 1/2 teaspoon / 2g. (yes)
Oregano dried 1/2 teaspoon / 2g. (yes)
Bay leaf 1 piece / 0,5g. (yes)
Peas, green 1/8 lbs - 2oz / 50g. (yes)
Onion (spring onion) 4 pieces / 80g. (yes)
Potato 1/4 lbs - 4oz / 100g. (yes)

**Cooking instructions:**
Sauce:
Tear off tomatoes and cut into small pieces. Reduce in a pot with a little olive oil, finely chopped garlic. Add 1 slice of dry toasted bread (crumbed), fresh finely grated Parmesan, finely chopped basil, oregano, salt and pepper.

Soup:
Boil the vegetable broth according to the basic recipe, add coarsely sliced carrots, diced celery, diced potatoes, small florets, broccoli, finely chopped fennel tuber, peas, thyme, oregano and the bay leaf. let cook 10 minutes.

Cut 4 scallions into thin rings, add them and cook another 2 min.

Pour sauce into a soup bowl. First only a few tablespoons. Stir boiling broth with it, then stir in the soup little by little.

## 9.82 Vegetable miso soup with tofu

Very powerful, strengthens after febrile illness, reduces blood pressure, strengthens immune system, prevents cancer, reduces radiation damage, improves blood circulation, strengthens liver and kidney, detoxifying, strengthens the muscles, reduces flatulence, forcing spleen.
Cooking time approx. 15 min
Allergens: EN
4 portions to 247,75g. / 107kcal. - (carb:22% / prot:78%)
100g.=43,09kcal. / protein 1,85g. fat:9,4g.
µg. - Ph:3,92 Na:13,88 Ka:10,98 Mg:1,98 Ca:4,08 Fe:0,07 Zn:0,01 Col.:0 Hsr.:1,45

**Quantity of ingredients:**
Sesame oil 2 table spoons / 35g. (yes)
Onion (shallot) 1 piece / 20g. (yes)
Carrot 1 piece / 70g. (yes)
Leek 2 inches / 10g. (yes)
Water 3 cups / 750g. (yes)
Endive salad 2 table spoons / 30g. (yes)
Soy Tofu 2 table spoons / 30g. (yes)
Ginger fresh 1/2 teaspoon / 1g. (yes)
Miso 2 table spoons / 15g. (yes)

**Cooking instructions:**
In sesame oil first sauté onions, then carrots and a little leek; Pour in water and simmer gently; add the bean sprouts and endive leaves and leave to stand; Tofu cubes, add a little ginger; at the end stir in a little cooled cooking-water the Miso.


## 9.83 Vegetable semolina soup

Diuretic, harmonizes the stomach and intestines, conducts bowel winds, reduces blood pressure, lowers cholesterol, detoxifying, good to fight loss of appetite, flatulence, inflammatory bowel disease, heartburn, twelffinger intestinal ulcers. Stimulates digestion, reduces pain.
Cooking time approx. 20 min
Allergens: AEGL
3 portions to 459,67g. / 199kcal. - (carb:79% / prot:21%)
100g.=43,22kcal. / protein 6,38g. fat:7,02g.
µg. - Ph:4,26 Na:4,63 Ka:23,27 Mg:6,33 Ca:22,08 Fe:0,09 Zn:0,04 Col.:0,39 Hsr.:2,88

**Quantity of ingredients:**
Basic recipe for a vegetable soup (nutritious) 2 cup / 500g. (yes)
Potato 1 piece / 80g. (yes)
Parsnip 1 piece / 180g. (yes)
Carrot 1 piece / 120g. (yes)
Celery root 3/8 lbs - 6oz / 150g. (yes)
Kohlrabi 1/2 piece / 200g. (yes)
Beans (green, fresh) 1/4 lbs / 100g. (yes)
Wheat semolina 2 table spoons / 24g. (yes)
Lovage 1/2 teaspoon / 2g. (yes)
Butter organic 1 table spoon / 20g. (little)
Soy sauce 1 teaspoon / 3g. (yes)

**Cooking instructions:**
Worm the prepared vegetable soup; cook the vegetables in the soup softly. Spread some wheatgrass and let it swell. At the end, add lovage-green and a little butter and taste with soy sauce.

## 9.84 Vegetarian vegetable-oatmeal-potatoes mash

Improves digestion, regenerates skin, supports urination, lowers cholesterol, supports urination, relieves constipation
Cooking time approx. 25 min
Allergens: A
2 portions to 109g. / 91kcal. - (carb:61% / prot:39%)
100g.=83,49kcal. / protein 1,89g. fat:4,42g.
µg. - Ph:13,11 Na:2,56 Ka:62,42 Mg:5,72 Ca:8,05 Fe:0,26 Zn:0,13 Col.:0 Hsr.:5,15

**Quantity of ingredients:**
Carrot (Early Carrot) 1 oz / 30g. (yes)
Parsnip 1 oz / 30g. (yes)
Zucchini 1 oz / 30g. (yes)
Fennel 1/2 oz / 10g. (yes)
Potato 1/8 lbs - 2oz / 50g. (yes)
Water 1/2 oz / 20g. (yes)
Oat flakes (whole grain) 1/2 oz / 10g. (yes)
Orange juice 1 oz / 30g. (little)
Rapeseed oil 1/4 oz / 8g. (yes)

**Cooking instructions:**
Wash the vegetables and potatoes, dice and fry in a little water. Add water and oatmeal, puree everything and finally add the oil. Note: This porridge replaces the vegetable-potato-meat porridge when meat is to be dispensed with in the infant's diet. Since meat is the best food

source for iron, a vegetarian diet must pay particular attention to a sufficient supply of iron.

## 9.85 Vitamin drink

Regulates gastrointestinal function, promotes spleen and liver, reduces blood pressure, strengthens immune system, prevents cancer, reduces radiation damage, supports urination, quenches thirst, calms the stomach, prevents cancer.
Cooking time approx. 5 min
3 portions to 273,33g. / 172kcal. - (carb:92% / prot:8%)
100g.=62,93kcal. / protein 2,78g. fat:0,57g.
µg. - Ph:9,44 Na:2,63 Ka:80,69 Mg:7,39 Ca:10,06 Fe:0,28 Zn:0,03 Col.:0 Hsr.:6,17

**Quantity of ingredients:**
Orange juice 1 cup / 300g. (little)
Carrot 5/8 oz / 200g. (yes)
Banana 2 pieces / 300g. (yes)
Kiwi 1 piece / 20g. (yes)

**Cooking instructions:**
Chop oranges, carrots, bananas and kiwi and finely puree with the blender.

## 9.86 Warming carrot soup

Strengthens and warms, reduces blood pressure, strengthens immune system, prevents cancer, reduces radiation damage, strengthens gastrointestinal function.
Cooking time approx. 30 min
Allergens: HL
3 portions to 274,67g. / 133kcal. - (carb:79% / prot:21%)
100g.=48,54kcal. / protein 2,16g. fat:7,86g.
µg. - Ph:2,86 Na:2,31 Ka:9,18 Mg:8,37 Ca:32,64 Fe:0,13 Zn:0,03 Col.:0 Hsr.:1

**Quantity of ingredients:**
Carrot 4 pieces / 250g. (yes)
Walnut oil 2 table spoons / 20g. (yes)
Onion (shallot) 2 pieces / 40g. (yes)
Anise (Common Fennel) 1/2 teaspoon / 1g. (yes)
Nutmeg 1 pinch / 1g. (yes)
Ginger fresh 1/2 teaspoon / 1g. (yes)
Salt 1 pinch / 1g. (little)
Basic recipe for a vegetable soup (nutritious) 2 cup / 500g. (yes)
Parsley 1 table spoon / 10g. (yes)

**Cooking instructions:**
Heat walnut oil in a hot pot and fry onions; steam the carrots in it; add anise, nutmeg, a little ginger, salt and sauté everything; add water or vegetable- or meat stock; cook everything soft and then puree; fold in parsley at the end.

Recommendation: Suitable for the cold season, especially if you use meat broth as a liquid for infusion.

## 9.87 Yogurt with honey and nuts

Relieves pain, detoxifying, promotes wound healing. Good to fight acute or chronic constipation of the intestine. Dissolves stones.
Cooking time approx. 5 min
Allergens: GH
1 portion to 167g. / 258kcal. - (carb:61% / prot:39%)
100g.=154,49kcal. / protein 6,79g. fat:12,43g.
µg. - Ph:107,54 Na:38,83 Ka:167,29 Mg:19,4 Ca:104,46 Fe:0,49 Zn:0,54 Col.:10,48
Hsr.:2,16

**Quantity of ingredients:**
Yogurt (natural, 3.5% fat) 1/4 lbs - 4oz / 125g. (yes)
Honey 2 table spoons / 30g. (little)
Walnuts 1 table spoon / 12g. (yes)

**Cooking instructions:**
Mix yoghurt with honey and finely chopped nuts.

# 10 Effects of food

## 10.1 Use ingredients: recommendable

Acai powder
Bitter Herb liqueur
Cream 10% coffee cream
Fox nut, gorgon nut, makhana
Hibiscus

Kudzu
Leaf salads (bitter)
Lettuce
Lily bulbs

## 10.2 Use ingredients: yes

Adzuki beans
Agar agar (kelp)
Agrimony
Almond
Almond milk
Almond puree
Aloe juice
Amaranth
Amaranth Pops
Anchovy / Sardine
Angelica root
Anise (Common Fennel)
Apple (sour)
Apple (sweet)
Apple puree
Apricot
Apricots
Arrowroot
Artichoke
Asparagus (green or white)
Aubergine
Baking powder
Balm
Bamboo shoots
Banana
Banana (cooking banana)
Banchatee (green tea)
barberry
Barley
Barley flour
Barley grass powder
Barley grouts
Barley malt
Barley not peeled
Basic recipe for a beef soup
Basic recipe for a beef soup (warming)
Basic recipe for a chicken soup
(warming)
Basic recipe for a duck soup
Basic recipe for a fish soup
Basic recipe for a rice soup (Congee)

Basic recipe for a vegetable soup
(nutritious)
Basil
Basil (fresh)
Batavia
Bay leaf
Bean oil
Beans (green, fresh)
Bearberry leaf
Beef bone marrow
Beef fillet
Beef heart
Beef heart (calf)
Beef lungs (calf)
Beef meat
Beef meat (calf)
Beef meatbones
Beef Oxtail pieces
Beef soup meat
Beef stomach
Berries of the season
Bitter orange peel
Black beans
Black caraway
Black fungus mushroom
Black tea
Blackberry dried (unripe fruit)
Blackberry leaves
Blackberry´s
Black-eyed peas
Blackthorn (Sloe)
Blue mallow tee
Blueberry
Blueberry dried
Bocksdorn fruits (Fructus Lycii, Goji,
goji berry dried
Boletus mushroom
Borage
Borage oil
Boxhorn clover seeds
Brazil nuts

Bread with carob kernel flour
Breadcrumbs (wheat bread, bread roll)
Brie cheese
Broad beans (thick beans)
Broccoli
Brussels sprouts
Buckbean
Buckwheat
Buckwheat (roasted) Kasha
Buckwheat whole grain
Bulgur (cereals)
Burdock root tea
Bush beans
Butter (half fat)
Butter beans white
Buttermilk
Camembert
Cantaloupe
Capers in olive oil
Carambola (Star fruit)
Cardamom
Carob flour, St. john's bread
Carp
Carrot
Carrot (Early Carrot)
Carrot juice without sugar
Cashews
Cauliflower
Caviar
Celery root
Celery sticks
Cereal coffee
Chamomile
Chamomile tea
Champignon
Channa-Dal
Chanterelle
Chard
Chenpi (chinese tangerine bowl)
Cherry
Cherry (sour)
Cherry compote
Chervil
Chervil dried
Chestnut puree
Chestnuts
Chicken Blood
Chicken egg
Chicken egg white
Chicken heart
Chicken meat
Chicken stomach
Chicken yolk
Chickpeas

Chickweed
Chicory
Chili (pod or ground)
Chinese cabbage
Chinese pearl barley
Chives
Chlorella (fresh water)
Chrysanthemum blossom tea
Cinnamon ground
Cinnamon sticks
Clementine
Clementines
Clove
Cocoa
Coconut flakes
Coconut grated
Coconut meat
Coconut milk
Codfish
Coffee
Coix (seeds) YiYi Ren
Cola drink (low calorie)
Compote (fruits of the season)
Cooking oil
Coriander
Coriander (fresh)
Corn
Corn (fast polenta)
Corn (roasted)
Corn flour
Corn germ oil
Corn Grease (Polenta)
Corn silk tea
Corn starch
Cottage cheese
Couscous
Cow's milk (1.5% fat)
Cow's milk (whole milk 3.5% fat)
Cranberries
Cranberry
Cranberry
Cranberry juice
Cream sour 10%
Creamer
Cress
Crispbread
Crucian
Cucumber
Cucumber (bitter)
Cucumber (spicy cucumber)
Cumin (Caraway seed)
Curcuma
Curd cheese 20%
Currant (black)

Currant (red)
Currant (white)
Currants (black)
Currants (red)
Curry
Curry paste red
Daisy
Dandelion (young plants)
Dandelion juice
Dandelionroots tea
Dashi
Dates red
Deer meat
Deer meat
Deer's Bones
Deer's kidneys
Dill
Duck (heart)
Duck (slaughtered)
Ducks egg
Dulse (seaweed)
Dyer's broom herb
Edam cheese
Elderberries
Elderberry blossom tee
Emmental cheese
Endive salad
Evening primrose oil
Fennel
Fennel seeds ground
Fennel tea
Fenugreek (Trigonella foenum-
graecum)
Feta cheese
Feta cheese
Fig
Fish innards
Fish pieces mixed (fresh water)
Fish remains
Fish sauce
Flounder
Flower pollen
French beans
Fresh cheese
Fresh cheese from soya
Fresh cheese with herbs
Freshwater crab
Freshwater fish
Fruit tea
Gail plum
Galangal
Garam Masala powder
Garlic
Gelatin white

Gelee Royal
Gentian root
Gentian root tea
Ginger fresh
Ginger oil
Ginger powder
Ginkgo fruit
Ginseng
Ginseng root
Goat
Goat and sheep's blood
Goat and sheep's brain
Goat and sheep's milk
Goat and sheep's stomach
Goat cheese
Goose blood
Goose egg
Gooseberry
Gouda cheese
Gourd
Grape juice red
Grape juice white
Grapefruit (Pomelo)
Grapefruit dried peel
Grapefruit juice
Grapeseed oil
Grass carp
Green spelt
Green tea
Greengage
Ground
Ground caraway
Guava
Hawthorn
Hazelnuts
Herbal tea mix
Herbs bitter
Herbs of Provence
Herbs various
Herbs wild
Hibiscus tea
Hijiki
Hokkaido pumpkin
Hop
Horehound leaves
Horse meat
Hyssop
Iceberg lettuce
Jasmine blossoms tee
Juniper berry
Kaki plum
Kalmus
Kefir
Kidney beans (red)

King Solomon's-seal
Kiwi
Kohlrabi
Kombu seaweed (Saccharina japonica)
Kukicha tea
Kumquats
Lamb bones
Lamb meat
Lamb shoulder
Lamb's lettuce
Lamb's lettuce
Lavender blossoms
Leek
Lemon
Lemon Balm (dried)
Lemon Balm (fresh)
Lemon juice
Lemon peel
Lemongrass
Lentils
Lentils black
Lentils red
Lentils yellow
Licorice root tea
Lima beans
Lime
Lime blossom tea
Linseed
Linseed (crushed)
Linseed oil
Liver smoothing tea
Longane
Loquate / Japanese medlar
Lotus roots
Lotus seeds
Lovage
Lovage seeds
Luo Han Guo fruit
Lychee
Lychee in Preserved
Lye roll
Mallow (Malva sylvestris) blossom tea
Malt
Mango
Manioc flour
Maple syrup
Mare's milk
Marjoram
Mediterranean fish (cod, plaice,
haddock, sea eel, mackerel)
Medlar
Millet
Millet flakes
Mineral water

Mirabelle plum
Miso
Miso black (fermented)
Miso paste (soy bean paste)
Mixed Pickles
Mold cheese
Morel (black, dried)
Morel, dried
Mozzarella
Mu Erh Mushroom
Muesli
Mulberry fruit
Mulled Wine Spice
Mullet
Multi-grain bread (gray bread)
Mung bean
Mung bean sprouting
Mustard
Mustard Dijon
Mustard medium hot
Mustard seeds
Mustard sweet
Mutton
Mutton
Nasturtium (nose-twister or nose-
tweaker)
Nectarine
Nettles
Noodles (wheat) with egg
Noodles (wheat, lasagne) with egg
Noodles (wheat, ribbon noodles) with
egg
Noodles (wheat, spaghetti) with egg
Noodles (whole grain) with egg
Nori, purple seaweed, red algae
Nutmeg
Oat
Oat flakes (whole grain)
Oat flakes roasted
Oat flour
Oat fusion (baby food)
Oat meal
Oat milk
Octopus
Okra
Olive oil
Olives
Olives green
Onion (shallot)
Onion (spring onion)
Onion read
Onion white
Orange
Orange blossom

Orange dried peel
Orange grated peel
Orange peel
Oregano dried
Oregano fresh
Oyster mushroom
Oyster shell powder
Oysters
Palm oil
Papaya
Parsley
Parsley root
Parsnip
Passion blossoms tea
Passion fruit
Peaches
Peaches (canned)
Peanut oil
Peanuts
Pear
Pearl barley
Pearl barley
Peas
Peas, green
Pepper (ground)
Pepper Cayenne
Pepper powder (hot)
Pepper white (ground)
Peppercorns
Peppermint
Peppermint tea
Pepperoni
Pepperoni, red, pitted, halved
Pepperoni, yellow, pitted, halved
Peppers
Peppers (rose peppers)
Peppers (sweet)
Peppers powder
Perch
Pheasant
Pickle
Pig blood
Pigeon
Pigeon egg
Pimento
Pine nuts
Pineapple
Pineapple (from a can)
Pineapple juice without sugar
Pinto beans speckled
Pistachios
Plaice
Plum
Plum dried

Plums
Pomegranate
Poppy
Pork Bacon
Pork brain
Pork ham
Pork ham cooked
Pork ham smoked
Pork heart
Pork knuckle
Pork lung
Pork marrow bones
Pork meat
Pork skin
Pork stomach
Pork/beef sausage (smoked)
Pork's intestine
Potato
Potato (mealy)
Potato flour
Prickly pear
Processed cheese 12%
Psyllium seed
Pudding powder vanilla
Pumpernickel (dark bread)
Pumpkin
Pumpkin seed oil
Pumpkin seeds
Quail
Quail egg
Quince
Quinoa
Rabbit
Rabbit (wild)
Rabbit meat
Radicchio
Radish
Radish (white, green, purple-red)
Radish black
Radish horseradish
Radish leaves
Rapeseed oil
Raspberry
Raspberry dried (immature)
Raspberry leaf tea
Red beet
Red berry (without sugar)
Red cabbage
Reishi mushroom
Rhubarb
Ribworttea
Rice (fragrance)
Rice (Gaoliang / Sorghum)
Rice (whole grain)

Rice Basmati
Rice black
Rice flour
Rice long grain rice
Rice malt
Rice mash
Rice noodles
Rice red
Rice round grain
Rice starch
Rice sticky
Rice sweet
Rice variety any
Rice wild (nature rice)
Romaine lettuce / lettuce salad
Rose blossom tea
Rose hip
Rose hip tea
Rose leaf tea
Rosefish
Rosemary
Rucola
Rusk
Rye
Rye flour
Rye wholemeal bread
Safflower (Dyer's thistle  / Hong Hua)
Saffron
Sage
Sago (cereals)
Salmon
Salsify
Sauerkraut (cutted cabbage fermented)
Savory
Savoy cabbage / kale
Sea buckthorn
Sea cucumber
Seacrab
Sesame oil
Sesame oil roasted
Sesame paste (Tahini)
Sesame, black
Sesame, white
Shark
Sheep's milk
Sheep's milk yoghurt
Shiitake, dried
Shrimp
Skim milk powder
Slug
Sorrel
Sour cherries
Sour milk
Sour milk cheese 20%

Sourdough
Soy flour
Soy noodles
Soy sauce
Soy Tofu
Soy Tofu smoked
Soya Cuisine (soy cream)
Soybean milk
Soybean oil
Soybeans
Soybeans, black
Soybeans, blacks, fermented
Soybeans, yellow
Spelled (Dark) bread
Spelled flakes
Spelled grain
Spelled semolina
Spelled wholemeal flour
Spinach
Spiny lobsters
Spurdog (spiny dogfish, Schillerlocken)
St. Benedict's thistle, blessed thistle,
holy thistle, spotted thistle
Star anise
Stevia (candyleaf, sweetleaf)
Strawberries
Sugar fructose - fruit sugar
Sugar glucose - grapes sugar
Sugar Milk Sugar
Sugar substitute (sweetener)
Sunflower oil
Sunflower seeds
Sweet potato
Tabasco
Tangerine
Tarragon (Estragon)
Tea mixture uric acid lowering
Thistle oil
Thyme
Thyme dried
Toast bread (whole grain)
Tomato
Tomato dried
Tomato juice
Tomato paste
Tomato puree
Tonic Water
Topinambur
Trout
Trout (smoked)
Truffle
Tsampa (roasted barley flour)
Tuna
Turkey breast meat

Turkey ham
Turmeric (yellow root)
Turnip
Turnips
Umeboshi paste
Umeboshi plums (Japanese apricots)
Valerian
Vanilla
Vanilla pod
Vanilla powder
Vegetable juice
Vinegar (Apple vinegar)
Vinegar (Red wine vinegar)
Vinegar Aceto Balsamico
Vinegar Aceto Balsamico white
Wakame
Walnut oil
Walnuts
Water
Water hot
Watermelon
Wax gourd
Wheat
Wheat bran
Wheat bulgur
Wheat flakes
Wheat flour
Wheat flour whole grain

Wheat germ oil
Wheat semolina
Wheat semolina for children
Wheat/Rye/Gray-black bread with yeast
Wheatgrass juice
Wheatgrass powder
Whey
White beans
White cabbage
Whitefish
Whole grain bread
Wholemeal flour
Wild boar meat
Wild garlic (garlic spinach)
Wild herbs
Wild strawberries
Wormwood herb
Yam root, yam root tuber
Yarrow
Yarrow tea
Yeast
Yew nut
Yoghurt vanilla
Yogi tea
Yogurt (natural, 1.5% fat)
Yogurt (natural, 3.5% fat)
Zucchini

## 10.3 Use ingredients: little

Acerola fruit nectar or powder
Agave nectar
Almond marzipan
Apple juice (natural cloudy)
Apricot dried
Apricot jam
Apricot nectar
Apricots juice
Avocado
Beef kidney
Beef liver
Beer (alcohol-free)
Beer (alcohol-reduced)
Berry juice
Bitter Lemon
Bitter liqueur
Blackberry jam
Blueberry jam
Blueberry juice
Bread roll
Butter organic
Cherry juice

Chicken liver
Chocolate
Chocolate (Diabetic)
Clarified butter
Coconut fat
Cola drink
Cranberry jam
Cream (30% fat)
Cream sour 20%
Cream sour 30%
Cream, sweet 30%
Créme fraiche cheese
Curd cheese 40%
Currant jam (black)
Currant jam (red)
Currant juice (black)
Dates dried
Eel
Eel smoked
Fig dried
Fructose (glucose)
Fruit mix juice

Goat and sheep's liver
Goose
Goose fat
Goose parts
Gorgonzola
Grapes red
Grapes white
Honey
Honey wine (Met)
Ladyfingers
Lamb kidneys
Lamb liver
Lychee liqueur
Mackerel
Mango juice
Margarine
Margarine (diet)
Mayonnaise 50%
Mayonnaise 80%
Orange jam
Orange juice
Parmesan
Peanut (roasted)
Peanut butter
Pear juice
Pork fat (lard)
Pork kidneys
Pork Lard
Pork liver

Pork sausage (Bratwurst)processed cheese 30%
Puff pastry
Rabbit liver
Raisins
Raspberry jam
Salt
Salt (herbal)
Sour cream 15% fat
Spirit
Strawberry jam
Strawberry Juice
Sugar - icing sugar
Sugar brown
Sugar candy white
Sugar cane sugar
Sugar molasses
Sugar palm sugar
Sugar white
Vanilla sugar natural
Walnuts roasted
Wheat flatbread/pita bread
White bread (baguette)
White bread (pretzel sticks)
White bread (roll)
White bread (wheat bread)
White breadcrumbs
White dumpling bread (wheat bread cut into chunks)

## 10.4 Do not use contra-acting foods

Beer (Pils)
Beer (Top-fermented German dark beer)
Brown ale
Calamari
Campari
Cod
Crab
Fernet Branca (herbal bitter liqueur)
Ginseng liqueur
Halibut (Flatfish)
Herring
Jellyfish
Lobster

Martini
Mussels
Octopus
Prosecco
Red wine
Rum
Sake
Sherry (whine)
Shrimps
Supplementary nutrition
Wheat beer
White wine
Wormwood

# 11 Complementary

## 11.1 Birch leaves

Folium Betulae
Preparation: Healing tea (infusion)
This tea is diuretic and helps against kidney ailments, gout and cleans the blood, also helps with bacterial and inflammatory urinary tract diseases, kidney grief and rheumatic complaints.
Dosage: Pour 2 tablespoons of crushed birch leaves into 250 ml of boiling water, let stand for 10 minutes. Then sieve.
Drink one cup of it a day.

## 11.2 Buckeye

Aesculus hippocastanum, fol.
Preparation: Different effects
Good for varicose veins, wrinkles, hemorrhoids, rheumatic complaints, menstrual problems, convulsions.
Dosage: Active ingredients: Aesculus saponins, tannins, flvonglycosides
Notice: Nit use in pregnancy, sensitive stomach.

## 11.3 Chili pods

Capsicum annuum, fruct.
Preparation: Embrocation
Externally as rubs well against rheumatic diseases, colds, fever, indigestion, nausea, vomiting, pain, depression, tension.
Dosage: Notice: High doses may lead to life-threatening hypothermia, prolonged use, acute gastritis, inflammation of the kidneys. Capsicum preparations irritate the skin and mucous membranes even in small quantities and may cause painful burning sensations.

## 11.4 Nettle leaves

Herba Urticae
Preparation: Healing tea (infusion)
Appetizing, Purifying, Hemostatic, Diarrhea, promotes blood formation, Promotes hair growth, Diuretic, Urinary tract disorders, Rheumatism, Expectorant, Metabolism, Rheumatism, Arthritis, Hypoglycemic, Detoxifying.
Dosage: Add 2-4 teaspoons of the tea to 250 ml of boiling water and infuse for 10 minutes. Then sieve. Drink 2 to 3 cups per day as needed.
Active Ingredients: Flavonoids, Chlorophylls, Vitamins, Mineral Salts,

Beta-Sistosterol, Plant Acid, Histamine in the Hair,

## 11.5 Reishi

Ganoderma lucidum
Preparation: Different effects
Regenerates the liver, has a detoxifying and anti-inflammatory effect.
Good for chronic hepatitis, swelling, redness and itching. Regulates the
immune system, awakens and supports the self-healing powers.
Improves the oxygen saturation of the blood.
Dosage: As an addition to tea, cocoa or coffee. As capsules, extract,
powder or whole mushroom.

## 11.6 Rooibos

Aspalathus linearis
Preparation: Healing tea (infusion)
Antioxidant, anti-inflammatory, anti-cancer, protects against flavanoids,
also has a positive effect on Alzheimer's, arteriosclerosis. Antiallergic,
inhibits histamine release. Antibacterial, antiviral, antifungal, detoxifying
(alkaline).
Dosage: Brew 3-4 teaspoons of rooibos with one liter of boiling water and
leave for 6-10 minutes. With soft water you need less tea for the
preparation, with harder water we recommend a higher dosage.

## 11.7 St. Benedict's thistle, blessed thistle, holy thistle

Centaurea benedicta
Preparation: Healing tea (infusion)
The oil of the plant, which has been used in purulent skin ulcers, has a
bacteriostatic action against staphylococci. Attention: The thistle has a
certain allergy potential.
Dosage: Notice: The Benedictine herb has a certain allergy potential. The
oil of the plant, which was used in purulent skin ulcers, acts
bacteriostatic especially against staphylococci.

# 12 Basics of Nutrition

The basic principles of nutrition described herein are general recommendations. They are not aimed at a specific form of therapy. Recommendations concerning a therapy have priority.

## 12.1 Nutrition

Regular meals in a relaxed atmosphere. A warm breakfast is considered a good start into the day.

The main meals ought to be taken for lunch – supper in the early evening. Pay attention to feeling hungry or sated: don't eat too much nor remain hungry is the rule

Prepare the meals freshly from natural, regional products. Frozen, heat-conserved, industrially prepared or foodstuffs cooked in the microwave oven are rejected.

Choice of foodstuffs according to the season: more cooling food in summer, more warming food in winter.

Eat cooked food at least twice a day. Food and drinks ought to be lukewarm, never ice-cold or hot.

Raw vegetables, briefly cooked vegetables, freshly squeezed juices and mineral water are not recommended. Milk and dairy products are only included in the diet if they don't cause problems.

Don't use therapeutic recipes over a longer period without consulting your doctor or therapist.

### Varied food

Enjoy the diversity of foodstuffs. Characteristics of a balanced nutrition are variety, suitable combination and a balanced quantity of rich and low energy foodstuffs (on one hand avoiding undersupply with essential nutrients and on the other hand to take to many undesirable substances).

### A lot of Cereal Products - and Potatoes

Bread, pasta, rice, cereal flakes (best wholemeal) as well as potatoes contain almost no fat, but many vitamins, mineral nutrients, trace elements, roughage and secondary plant substances. These foodstuffs ought to be taken with low-fat side dishes.

### Vegetables and Fruit – „Take Five" every day ...

5 portions of vegetables and fruit a day, as fresh as possible, briefly cooked, or maybe one portion as a juice – ideal as a side dish to every meal as well as snack between meals: Thus a lot of vitamins, mineral nutrients as well as roughage and secondary plant substances

### Daily milk and dairy products
Milk and Dairy Products every Day, once or twice per Week Fish; meat, sausages as well as eggs moderately. These foodstuffs contain valuable nutrients like calcium in the milk, iodine selenium and omega-3 fat acids in saltwater fish. Meat is favorable due to its high content of disposable iron and the vitamins B1, B6 and B12. Quantities of 300 – 600 g meat and sausage per week are sufficient. Prefer low-fat products, especially in meat- and dairy products.

### Low-fat and fatty Foodstuffs
Fat supplies us with essential fat acids and fatty foodstuffs contain also fat-soluble vitamins. Fat is high in energy; therefore much fat in the food may cause overweight, possibly also cancer. Too many saturated fat acids may further a tendency for cardio-vascular diseases in the long term. Prefer vegetable oils and fats (e.g. rapeseed-, olive-, soya-oils and solid fats produced therefrom). Beware of invisible fat in meat- and dairy products, pastry and sweets as well as in fast-food and convenience foods. 70 – 90 g fat per day is sufficient.

### Moderately Sugar and Salt
Take sugar and foods/drinks containing various kinds of sugar (e.g. glucose syrup) only occasionally. Use herbs and spices as well as a little salt creatively. Prefer salt containing iodine.

### Plenty of Liquids
Water is absolutely essential. Drink 1-2 l liquids every day. Prefer water (with or without gas) and other low-calorie drinks. Alcoholic drinks should not be taken.

### Tasty Dishes, carefully cooked
Cook the meals with as low temperatures and as short as possible, using little water and fat – this preserves the original taste, keeps the nutrients intact and prevents the production of harmful compounds.

### Take time and enjoy the food
Take your Time and enjoy your Food
Eating consciously helps to eat right. The eye enjoys food, too. It's fun, invites to enjoy varied dishes and stimulates the feeling of satiety.

### Watch your Weight and stay in Motion
A balanced diet and a lot of exercise and sport (30 – 60 min/day) are a healthy combination. The right weight furthers well-being and health. Thermals, directional effectiveness, digestive power

There are various criteria for judging the effectiveness of herbs and foodstuffs.

The use of certain herbs and ingredients is based on observations of the effects on the body which these foodstuffs, herbs and spices show after having eaten them. The medical science has developed following system: Every ingredient or herb has a directional effectiveness. Furthermore, there are herbs which have a special effect on certain organs.

The basic condition for a healthy metabolism is to obtain sufficient energy from food and that the digestive process doesn't use too much energy. An easily digestible meal makes content and sated, doesn't cause flatulence and fatigue after the meal. The perfect spices increase the healthiness of our meals. Very often, just small doses of herbs and spices will suffice. They are not used to make us sated, but to help our digestive organs to digest the food.

## 12.2 Recipes

The recipes list the ingredients to be used and the cooking instructions show how the dish is prepared. The list of ingredients shows the concerned quantities as well as the relevance for the therapy. If you find „less than mentioned", try to comply or find an alternative from the „list of recommended foodstuffs". Mostly it shall result just in a small change of taste when you simply avoid this ingredient.

Mild cooking methods: boiling, stewing, poaching, steaming
Strong cooking methods: barbecuing, roasting, frying, smoking
Balanced cooking methods: deep-frying, baking brick
Deep-freezing and warming in the microwave oven should be avoided (denaturalization).

## 12.3 Foodstuffs

Foodstuffs have an effect on body and soul like medicinal herbs, only a very much milder one. Dietary advice is mainly based on regional foodstuffs. The knowledge about the effects of each foodstuff and the knowledge, when which foodstuff shall be used, is based on the orthodoschool of medicine. Use ecologic-organic products, if possible. As everything should be cooked for a long time due to a better digestability and very rarely eaten raw, the food agrees with everyone.

The classification of the foodstuffs according to their effect on the body is the basis in order to achieve a harmonious status of health.

Dietary advisors do not recommend certain foodstuffs for everyone. The individual diet is tailor-made for the individual constitution.

Buy only fresh and ripe fruit and vegetables. You ought to leave unripe fruit and vegetables and such with brown spots and wilted leaves behind in the market. In this case take deep-frozen goods (never ready-to-serve dishes!). Fruit and vegetables are deep-frozen immediately after harvesting and often contain more vitamins and minerals than the goods from the vegetable shelf. Whereas conserved or tinned goods contain very much less biological substances. Also, salt, sugar and others are mostly added to the latter. Never leave the foodstuffs in the water after washing them to avoid that many vital substances get drowned. Clean salads, fruit and vegetables immediately before serving.

Please make sure of the hygienic processing of foodstuffs. Clean your salads, fruit and vegetables carefully. When cooking with meat, prepare all ingredients first and then process the meat products. Clean the worktop and tools very carefully. Wooden surfaces ought to be treated with a mild disinfectant regularly in order to reduce germination.

Store fruit and vegetables separately, if possible. Harvested fruit and vegetables are still alive and emit e.g. ethylene gas, which makes other products ripen and age faster. Keep meat and fish in the closed packaging or store them in the fridge in closed containers.

## 12.4 Herbs

There are some basic rules for storing medicinal herbs. On principle, herbs must be protected from direct sunlight, humidity and heat.

Containers for the storage of herbs may be glasses, ceramic jars and even plastic containers. However, plastic is a rather unsuitable material and should only be a short-term solution. In case of glass containers, use a dark material.

Medicinal herbs cannot be kept for any long period. The shelf life of herbs is limited. However, it can be prolonged with suitable storage. The place should be dark, rather cool and absolutely dry. A wooden medicine cabinet, placed not directly next to a source of heat, would be ideal. Never buy large quantities of herbs so as not to have to throw them away. Label the container with the name of the herb and the date of harvesting or processing.

# 13 Other dietic-books

The following syndromes of dietetics, TCM or for a therapy supplement for cancer are available.

## Dietetics

E001. Nutrition of the infant - baby food
E002. Nutrition during lactation
E003. Nutrition in old age
E004. Nutrition of children and adolescents
E005. Nutrition of athletes
E006. Light weight
E007. Pregnancy
E008. Full food

**Protein and electrolyte - kidneys**
E009. (hemodialysis) dialysis treatment
E010. Acute renal failure
E011. Chronic renal insufficiency
E012. Nephrotic syndrome
E013. Kidney stones (nephrolithiasis)

**Gastrointestinal tract - pancreas**
E014. Acute pancreatitis (inflammation of the pancreas)
E015. Chronic pancreatitis (inflammation of the pancreas)

**Gastrointestinal tract - small intestine and large intestine**
E016. Acute obstipation (constipation)
E017. Chronic obstipation (constipation)
E018. Colon irritabile
E019. Diverticulitis
E020. Acquired lactose intolerance (lactose malabsorption)
E021. Fructose malabsorption
E022. Glutensensitive enteropathy (celiac disease)
E023. Colectomy
E024. Short Bowel Syndrome

**Gastrointestinal tract - liver, gallbladder, bile ducts**
E025. Acute and chronic hepatitis (inflammation of the liver)
E026. Cholelithiasis (bile stones)
E027. fatty liver
E028. cirrhosis

**Gastrointestinal tract - Stomach and duodenal intestine**
E029. Acute gastritis
E030. Chronic gastritis
E031. Stomach bleeding
E032. Ulcus ventriculi and duodenal ulcer
E033. Condition after gastric surgery

### Gastrointestinal tract - oral cavity and esophagus
E034. Stomatitis
E035. Esophageal carcinoma (esophageal cancer)
E036. Refluosophagitis (heartburn)

### Special diseases
E037. Phenylketonuria (PKU)
E038. Rheumatic joint diseases

### Metabolism
E039. Obesity (overweight)
E040. Diabetes mellitus
E041. Eating disorders (underweight)

### Fat metabolism
E042. Hypercholesterolaemia (increased cholesterol level)
E043. Hepatic Encephalopathy

### Heart and circulation
E044. Arteriosclerosis (arterial calcification)
E045. Heart insufficiency
E046. Hypertension
E047. Hyperuricaemia and gout

### Changed nutrient requirements
E048. In case of fever
E049. For malignant diseases
E050. After burns
E051. Radiation and chemotherapy

## CANCER
E100. Pancreatic cancer
E101. Bladder cancer
E102. Blood cancer (leukemia)
E103. Breast cancer
E104. Colorectal cancer
E105. Gastric cancer
E106. Kidney cancer
E107. Esophageal cancer

## TCM
E200. Bladder - moisture heat in the bladder
E201. Bladder - moisture and cold in the bladder
E202. Bladder - emptiness and cold in the bladder
E203. Large intestine - external cold affects the large intestine
E204. Large intestine - moisture heat in the large intestine
E205. Large intestine - heat blocks the intestine II acute
E206. Large intestine - dryness of the colon
E207. Large intestine - Yang deficiency (cold)
E208. Heart - Blood insufficiency
E209. Heart - Blood stagnation
E210. Heart - Fire
E211. Heart - Hot mucus clogs the heart pores

E212. Heart - Cold mucus clogs the heart pores
E213. Heart - Qi deficiency
E214. Heart - Yang deficiency
E215. Heart - Yin deficiency
E216. Liver - Ascending Liver Yang
E217. Liver - Blood deficiency
E218. Liver - Blood stagnation
E219. Liver - Moisture heat in liver and gall bladder
E220. Liver - Fire
E221. Liver - Gall bladder Qi-Empty
E222. Liver - Cold in the liver meridian
E223. Liver - Qi stagnation
E224. Liver - Wind
E225. Liver - Wind with ascending liver Yang
E226. Liver - Wind with blood anemic
E227. Liver - Wind with extreme heat
E228. Lung - Qi deficiency
E229. Lung - Mucus-moisture in the lungs
E230. Lung - Mucus-heat in the lungs
E231. Lung - Mucus-cold in the lungs
E232. Lung - Dryness of the lungs
E233. Lung - Wind-heat attacks the lungs
E234. Lung - Wind-cold affects the lungs
E235. Lung - Yin deficiency
E236. Stomach - Bloodstagnation
E237. Stomach - Fire
E238. Stomach - Cold with liquid
E239. Stomach - Nutrition stagnation
E240. Stomach - Qi deficiency
E241. Stomach - Rebellious Qi
E242. Stomach - Yin Emptiness
E243. Spleen - Heat and moisture attack the spleen
E244. Spleen - Coldness and moisture affects the spleen
E245. Spleen - Qi deficiency
E246. Spleen - Qi deficiency + Declining spleen Qi
E247. Spleen - Qi deficiency + spleen does not control the blood
E248. Spleen - Yang deficiency
E249. Kidney - Heart and kidney no longer communicate
E250. Kidney - Jing deficiency
E251. Kidney - Kidneys cannot receive the Qi
E252. Kidney - Qi is not stable
E253. Kidney - Yang deficiency
E254. Kidney - Yin deficiency


For further information visit di-book.com.

# 14 EBNS - Software for nutritional counseling

The main task of the database is to create personalized nutritional advice for each patient individually. The database was developed for Dietetics and Traditional Chinese Medicine.

The Database supports training and advices in the daily work routine.

The computer program provides lists of recipes, ingredients and herbs, which are given to the client. individually adjustable according to patient's request from whole food to vegetarians (lacto, ovo, ...). For every register there is an information sheet which can be given to the client. All texts can be individually designed.

The syndromes can be combined and result in an intersection of the recommended recipes and ingredients. The automated diagnosis for the TCM enables you to check your experience during the training as well as to confirm your diagnosis in the working day. You select several predefined symptoms and have the program automatically display the relevant syndromes.

How to work with the database:
Select the patient / client, select one or more of the syndromes you diagnosed and print the folder.

You can change all values, create new symptoms or syndromes, develop recipes, change or adapt ingredients and herbs to your findings. In simple client management, all relevant data about the person is stored. You get an overview of the past diagnoses and the development of the course of the disease.

As a consultant you save a lot of time when you print out the recipe, food and herbal lists for the recognized syndromes and give them to the clients. You can use this time for a personal conversation. With the database, dieticians and nutritionists can view the nutrients and trace elements for each recipe and develop recipes for syndromes even with suggested ingredients.

All recipe and grocery lists can also be ordered from me as a combination of several diseases. I wish all readers good luck, health and happiness in life.
More information can be found at www.ebns.at.
Volunteer: www.krebsinfo.at
Josef Miligui